JUL 1 3 2009

EAST MEADOW PUBLIC LIBRARY

3 1299 00807 0592

D1174476

East Meadow Public Library
1886 Front Street
East Meadow, New York 11554
516-794-2570
www.eastmeadow.info

What people said about the first edition of *How Much Is Enough?*

"The best book I have ever read on money, happiness, and the steps you can take to achieve your dreams. With simple explanations, easy-to-follow suggestions, and a gentle grace, the authors guide you along the path to greater self-understanding and enhanced well-being. It is an outstanding book. Read it and you will live a happier life."
—Dr. Richard L. Peterson, founder, Market Psychology Consulting, and author of *Inside the Investor's Brain: The Power of Mind over Money*

"Simply put, this is a GREAT book to read, but you'll find it's even a BETTER book to use. As I read it, I found myself wishing I had written it myself."
—Doug Lennick, CFP, CEO, Lennick Aberman Group, and coauthor of *Moral Intelligence: Enhancing Business Performance and Leadership Success*

"The authors open a whole new world that ties the psyche to the state of our finances. *How Much Is Enough?* is more than any guidebook found on the shelves of the self-help section. Its outstanding quality is the depth at which it explores the tie between mental choices and the decisions that govern our financial status . . . the ideas that have been introduced challenge the way we see money and proffer a guide to maximize our wealth potential."
—*MillionaireAsia*, January 2008

"Fascinating and challenging. I've read it from cover to cover and can't stop thinking about it. I've determined to buy it for each of my children."
—Dr. Rosemary Howell, chairman, Strategic Action Pty. Ltd.

"Threatens to have long-lasting and far-reaching consequences for financial planning."
—*Sydney Morning Herald*, November 17, 2007

"Wonderful insights into the role of money, happiness, and how to lead a meaningful life."
—Raymond Ackerman, founder, Pick 'n Pay, and author of
  Hearing Grasshoppers Jump

"Conveys a central message. Work from the inside out. Financial success is only one part of a multifaceted person. Knowing what is important to you is the first thing you need to know; getting the resources to achieve that ultimate goal is just a supporting role. There is the need for the earnest pursuit of a different type of capital. Happiness Capital."
—*Wealth*, September 2007

"Thought-provoking and ultimately uplifting—I will be permanently better off for having read it."
—James O'Loughlin, author of *The Real Warren Buffett*

"Abey and Ford delve into the reasons why even though we're living longer, are richer and have more choices than ever before, many of us fail to choose things in life that make us truly happy. This practical guide uses interesting real life case studies to illustrate its teachings . . . not only will this book inspire you, it will guide you through practical strategies to enable you to live your dream."
—*The Finder*, September 2007

How Much Is Enough?

MAKING FINANCIAL DECISIONS THAT
CREATE WEALTH *and* WELL-BEING

Arun Abey
& Andrew Ford

GREENLEAF
BOOK GROUP PRESS

Authors' note: This book provides general information about money, investment, and people's attitudes toward these subjects. Every effort has been made to ensure that the contents of the book are accurate at the time of publication. Investment markets and the factors that drive them are constantly changing, however. Information in the book is in no way intended to replace or supersede independent or other professional advice. Neither the authors nor the publisher may be held responsible for any action or claim resulting from the use of this book or any information contained in it. References to dollars, unless otherwise specified, are to U.S. dollars.

The various case studies and stories of people's lives are drawn from real-life experiences that in some cases involve composite stories. People's names have been changed in these stories to protect their privacy.

Published by Greenleaf Book Group Press
Austin, TX
www.greenleafbookgroup.com

First edition published 2007 by A&B Publishers Pty. Ltd. atf A&B Trust, Australia

Copyright ©2009 by Arun Abey and Andrew Ford
All rights reserved under all copyright conventions.
No part of this book may be reproduced, stored in a retrieval system, or transmitted by any means, electronic, mechanical, photocopying, recording, or otherwise, without written permission from the publisher.

Distributed by Greenleaf Book Group LLC
For ordering information or special discounts for bulk purchases, please contact Greenleaf Book Group LLC at PO Box 97869, Austin, TX 78709, (512) 891-6100.

Design and composition by Greenleaf Book Group LLC
Cover design by Greenleaf Book Group LLC
Publisher's Cataloging-In-Publication Data
(Prepared by The Donohue Group, Inc.)

Abey, Arun.
    How much is enough? : making financial decisions that create wealth and well-being / Arun Abey & Andrew Ford. -- 2nd ed.

    p. : charts ; cm.

Previous ed. published: [Sydney], Australia : A&B Publishers Pty Ltd atf A&B Trust, 2007.
Includes bibliographical references and index.
ISBN: 978-1-929774-83-8

1. Finance, Personal. 2. Investments. I. Ford, Andrew (Andrew Robert James), 1968- II. Title.

HG179 .A249 2009
332.024/01   2008944175

Part of the Tree Neutral™ program, which offsets the number of trees consumed in the production and printing of this book by taking proactive steps, such as planting trees in direct proportion to the number of trees used: www.treeneutral.com

Printed in the United States of America on acid-free paper
09 10 11 12 13 14   10 9 8 7 6 5 4 3 2
Second Edition

To our clients around the world,
who have given us their trust and
the privilege of sharing in their life dreams

CONTENTS

ACKNOWLEDGMENTS

Since the publication of the first edition of *How Much Is Enough?* we have spent countless hours discussing, further researching, and making presentations to a range of audiences on the themes of money and well-being raised in the book. We have been pleased by the strong level of reader engagement we have received and the personal stories that have been shared openly. It seems we are not the only ones asking, and attempting to answer, the question "How much is enough?"

While many of these letters and conversations have been private, one of the most memorable was from an executive who had that morning taken a break from his hectic schedule to walk his young daughter to school for the first time in months. He had then taken the trouble to e-mail us to explain how much this simple act had meant to him—and to his daughter. We would like to thank each of these correspondents and, where possible, we have incorporated their insights into the text of this revised and fully updated edition.

This edition also features an additional chapter titled "Kids, Money, and Happiness." Parents of young children in particular have asked for more information on the fascinating challenge of inculcating in our children a healthy respect for the important role that money can play in life, combined with an appreciation of the importance of personal values and goals to well-being. In short, most readers seem to want their kids to understand that while money matters a great deal, at the end of the day it is an "enabler." Provided you have sufficient money to cover the basic necessities in life, there are in fact more important things to aim for.

Many people have helped to make this book what it is. Shlomo Benartzi spent considerable time reviewing content and providing useful suggestions to make it more accessible. Ross Ackland, Brett Nan Tie, James Murray, Melanie Nutbeam, Chloe Yildiz, and Patrick Au-Yeung provided essential research assistance. Bernie Bolger shared valuable insights and personal experience, as well as assisted with the research.

The following individuals also provided valuable comments: Shaun Bonnét, Andrew Bradley, Jon Brett, Walter Carpenter, Paul Clitheroe, John Dani, Harold Evensky, Tanya Ford, Susan Foster, Letetia Gibbs, Tony Gilding, Tony Green, Peeyush Gupta, Jenny Hill-Ling, Peter Janssen, Helen Jones, Antony Kidman, Anthony Kongats, Helen Lynch, Alan McCormack, Andrew Penn, Mark Peterie, Geoff Roberts, Cliff Rosenberg, Tim Sharp, Duff Watkins, and Heidl Wolter.

Vicki Jackson and Shabnum Stevens assisted with typing, graphics, and logistics.

Linda O'Doughda was a vigilant and effective editor, and Bill Crawford also provided important input.

ipac securities provided considerable production support, and so many colleagues at ipac and AXA provided help and encouragement that it would be impossible to name them all. Their help was nonetheless greatly appreciated. Any errors or omissions are of course our responsibility.

Last, but most important, our families provided the love, encouragement, and practical support that enabled us to keep the faith despite the long period of time taken to complete the book.

—Arun Abey and Andrew Ford
   Spring 2009

FOREWORD

IF YOU SERIOUSLY CONSIDER THE QUESTION, reflecting on the title alone—*How Much Is Enough?*—would justify owning this book. As Arun and Andrew so pointedly note in the first few pages, as a society we have become far richer in the past fifty years but we have not become happier! Obviously, we need to step back and consider this sad reality. The authors have a passion, and that passion is to ensure that when we look back ten and twenty years from now, we will be happier. This book provides the ideas, suggestions, tips, and strategies for assisting us in moving both practically and emotionally onto the right path to win the Happiness Prize.

In her books, my partner, Deena Katz, tells the story of her mom (and others of her generation) who bought a refrigerator when she needed one. Today we buy one when we want one. No money, no problem; just get a loan. How depressing. No wonder we're not happier. How did we get here? *How Much Is Enough?* alerts us to the fact that consumer marketing is increasingly focused on ensuring that we are dissatisfied with what we have and who we are. It then proceeds to introduce the concept of hedonistic opportunity cost, that is, a measure of happiness foregone. This is a powerful tool that reframes our focus from price to utility. The simple example provided by the authors, "think of the cost of a much more expensive car in terms of, say, the additional happiness that a family holiday overseas ... may have produced," is just one example of the multitude of tidbits that we can immediately incorporate into our daily lives.

Although it's impossible to highlight one part of the book as most important, following their powerful introductory sections on foundations and "the meaning of money," the authors address one issue of supreme interest to many of us: kids, money, and happiness. Noting that research has consistently shown that money habits are generally inculcated before a child's tenth birthday, this section jump-starts our efforts to set our children on the path to happiness. In fact, one of my favorite ideas is the Family Bank, but you'll have to read the book to see why.

Another discussion, perhaps obvious in hindsight but one we all too often forget, is the reminder that the "Ultimate Prize is to move from a life that is successful for you, to a life that is also meaningful to others." If the book simply reminded us of this reality, it would be useful; however, as with each chapter, it goes far beyond a wake-up call; it provides ideas and strategies that enable us to creatively implement giving with meaning. In fact, I've already changed my holiday gifting plans based on what I learned.

As one would expect of a book coauthored by a leading strategic thinker and the founder of ipac, one of the world's largest financial planning companies, investments play a big role in the story of *How Much Is Enough?* However, unlike all too many investment guides, this book is well founded in both solid investment theory and real-world practicality. Recognizing that the critical "difference between success and failure is not how investment markets behave . . . but how investors behave," the authors introduce the reader to the lessons of behavioral finance. You'll learn about the dangers of loss aversion and investment regret and the concepts of time horizons and risk premium. What you learn will increase your likelihood of winning the Investment Prize. Even then, as a practitioner, I'm obviously biased, and I believe that investors are well served by good professional advice. So, I was pleased to find a very solid chapter on evaluating and selecting good advisers.

I could go on and on, but I would still not do credit to this most important volume. With the overriding theme that we need to focus on our life, not our money in order to win the Happiness Prize, *How Much Is Enough?*

delivers on its promise to assist you, the reader, "to improve not just your bank balance but your life balance."

—Harold Evensky, CFP, President, Evensky & Katz
Author of *Wealth Management* and coeditor of *The Investment Think Tank*
and *Retirement Income Redesigned*, Adjunct Professor, Texas Tech University

INTRODUCTION:
RICHER AND HAPPIER

EACH ONE OF US WANTS TO BE HAPPY AND HAVE ENOUGH MONEY, and the good news is that today's world offers the opportunity for both. By planning, taking some simple, practical steps, and—above all—becoming master of your mind, you *can* have it all.

Thanks to advances in technology, medicine, and other fields during the past hundred years, we're living longer, healthier, and wealthier lives. We have more choices too. In fact, most people now have an unprecedented array of options in everything from education and career to housing, medical treatment, and retirement. Fortunately, we also have the financial potential to exploit the choices available to us.

With as little as $1,000 we can access a professionally managed portfolio holding investments around the globe. We can own a stake in the world's best companies, lend money to the world's most reliable governments—charging interest, of course—or collect rents from any number of impressive properties in equally impressive locations. All of this can be done without risking large amounts of capital and without the kind of backbreaking effort required in the past to become wealthy.

The result is that we can enjoy the best of all possible worlds: better health and longevity, more choices, and enough money to make the most of it.

ARE WE MAXIMIZING OUR POTENTIAL?

Our potential to achieve wealth and well-being is practically unlimited, so how well are we doing? Are we maximizing our potential, or could we do better?

Many people enjoy life a great deal and some experience genuine fulfilment, so we're doing some things right. But as a community, even though we have become far richer over the past fifty years as measured by our economic output and rising incomes, we have not become happier.

Happiness surveys conducted globally have repeatedly shown a plateau in human happiness at a modest level of household income. It also appears that an increasing number of us are falling through the cracks.

- Youth and adult suicide rates have doubled or tripled over the past forty years.
- The biggest-selling drugs are those treating depression, anxiety, and stress.
- The onset of depression now occurs at age fourteen, anxiety at age eleven.
- Obesity and diabetes have reached epidemic proportions.

To a greater or lesser extent, these problems are experienced across all Western countries and socioeconomic strata. We know something is terribly wrong when one of the 220,000 Web resources dealing with teen suicide bluntly states, "Today's teenagers know a lot more than their parents in terms of technology, but they have also achieved something their parents' generation did not—they are killing themselves far more than any other generation." Our happiness scorecard should be better.

Not only has rising wealth failed to make human beings happier, it has also failed to ensure our personal financial security. While many individuals enjoy freedom from financial worries, the majority of people worldwide do not. Baby boomers, the first generation to enjoy the prospect of a long and healthy retirement, typically have underprepared and undersaved, and they are anxious about having enough money in old age. While living longer is a blessing, it correspondingly means that we need to find a way to pay for new opportunities over a much longer period.

Research by Professor Robert Cummins and his colleagues at Deakin University in Melbourne, Australia, has revealed that the distress people feel in relation to income uncertainty (even to a small degree) reduces well-being more powerfully than does strong physical pain.

Having a high income, however, does not necessarily solve the problem of maximizing our financial resources and making our money last. Executives on six-figure incomes in many countries still report that they spend more than they earn.

Compounding the problem is the fact that we do not invest our savings well. The stock market offers an excellent prize for long-term investing, yet investors in the market capture only about one-quarter of the available returns. Our financial scorecard should be better.

IMPROVING OUR SCORECARDS

The simple fact is, our happiness and financial scorecards are not as good as they could be because we are not well equipped to thrive in this new environment. The opportunities available to us are so new that we need to employ new skills and new ways of thinking to take advantage of them.

The key to overcoming these challenges and simultaneously improving our happiness and our money scorecards is a disarmingly simple idea: You are what you think.

Developing a greater understanding of how you think, why you think that way, and what you can do about it are central to leading a better life. *How Much Is Enough?* helps you get started. It provides a framework for understanding the relationship between money and happiness that's right for you, and for bringing more of both into your life.

Even if you do nothing to maximize your wealth and well-being, the chances are you will still live better than earlier generations. But if you want the best out of life, if you want to make more money and have more fun, you'll need to plan for both financial and personal success.

To make this planning worthwhile, you'll need to answer the question "How much is enough?" How much is enough money? How much is enough time with your family? How much is enough time to pursue your passions? How much is enough to balance all areas of your life to achieve fulfilment?

DOES MONEY BRING HAPPINESS, OR DOES HAPPINESS BRING MONEY?

Money is commonly sought as a shortcut to happiness. That's because although the human brain has evolved, it hasn't changed as quickly as the world around us has. As a result, we look for shortcuts. The sheer number of possible choices, and the stress of weighing them, can cause us to throw our hands up in despair and follow what seems a sure formula: money = happiness. This well-worn path often leads to disappointment, however; sometimes we find that having more money and more choices makes us less happy.

How many people focus on earning higher degrees and certifications to maximize their income, then build a career on the assumption that once money is made, happiness will follow? How many people think, "Once I have that new house/that new car/that new yacht, then I'll be happy"? While these things can be nice, as the unhappy rich could tell you, the pursuit of wealth for its own sake is unlikely to yield anything more significant than a new (presumably) bigger house, car, or yacht.

It would be ridiculous to say that all rich people are unhappy, however. When money helps us to live in a way that's consistent with our values and goals, it can play a direct role in promoting happiness. But to achieve this we need to figure out what makes us tick. What are our values and goals? We need to work out who we are and what will give us a sense of well-being.

Strangely enough, understanding what makes us happy often leads to greater financial success as well. This is because we are more likely to be engaged and productive in our work and in managing our money, creating opportunities for success that would not otherwise be available to us. Happiness brings money rather than the other way around.

So how can we ensure that money makes a positive contribution to our sense of well-being, rather than being a source of anxiety? By planning ahead, being smart about money, and having adequate insurance to protect against the unexpected, you're on the way to taking care of your financial health. But will you also be on the way to well-being? How can you avoid the ranks of the unhappy rich and find both wealth and personal well-being? That's where *How Much Is Enough?* will help you.

CAUTIONARY FABLES

The Greedy Monkey

Sir Isaac Newton, one of the fathers of modern science, is somewhat less well known as a share investor. Newton was not given to idleness, so when he came into a substantial inheritance, he put his wealth to work.

At that time, in the early 1700s, the South Sea Company was all the rage among gentlemen who traded in stocks and shares. Newton bought shares in the group, which was formed, ostensibly, to trade in the Caribbean, South America, and the Pacific "South Seas." Its real purpose, however, was to convert British government debt into common stock that would be held by the masses.

Newton followed his peers and bought shares in the company. In the spring of 1720, its share price began to soar for no reason that anyone could identify. Speculative mania drew in everyone from professional investors to ladies who sold their jewels.

Observing this phenomenon, Newton commented, "I can calculate the motions of the heavenly bodies, but not the madness of people." One of history's greatest thinkers and a religious man, he frowned on the hordes of "lucky fools." So, he sold his shares, originally valued at £7,000, at a tidy 100 percent profit. And that should have been that.

The mania continued, however, and as others piled in, the price of South Sea Company shares surged. Surely Newton would demonstrate the discipline and fortitude to ride out the feelings of disappointment and envy that such situations can arouse?

Sadly, the answer is that he did not. He reentered the market close to its peak, making an even larger investment. Shortly afterward, the stock price burst like a bubble (hence the name given to the episode, the South Sea

Bubble), and Newton lost £20,000 in the collapse. He hadn't paid heed to his very own principle: What goes up must come down.

As Charles Kindleberger remarked in his classic account of the episode, "In the irrational habit of many of us who experience disaster, [Newton] put it out of his mind, and never, for the rest of his life, could he bear to hear the name South Sea."

Intelligence is no guarantee of success. Newton was distracted by the actions of others—rather than following his own path. Because it involves reacting to the behavior of others, such a strategy has as little chance of success as a stint behind the poker machine.

The Thrifty Squirrel

Mr. and Mrs. Bill Kempton married in 1950 in middle-class Middleton, where they took pride in being meticulously prudent and modest. They were good at saving: in fact, they accumulated a small fortune over the years.

Bill Kempton distrusted all financial institutions and kept his money under the bed.

Mary Kempton, who was a little more practical, convinced her husband that opening a savings account with the biggest bank was a more rational thing to do: it paid some interest, and the bank was there forever, surely.

Decades came and went, with the Kempton money safely tucked away in the savings account at the biggest bank in Middleton. When Bill Kempton passed away of old age, Mary Kempton decided to pass on the savings to her niece, Emma, her only relative. She strolled to the bank and politely asked for her money.

Sadly, their fortune was no more. The ravages of inflation had depleted Mary Kempton's generous gift to a pittance. Back in 1950, the savings would have bought a three-bedroom family home in a decent suburb. Sixty years later, however, it wasn't enough for a deposit on a one-bedroom house. Bill and Mary Kempton let fear and indecision distract them from the important task of clearly defining what they hoped to achieve with their money. In the confusing world of investment, as in life, they took the safe route: big bank, low interest. Cruelly, this can be the safest route to long-term ruin.

The Hungry Hound

James Morley grew up knowing that his place was at the top. No one was surprised, least of all him, that he won an academic scholarship to Harvard, or that the very best Wall Street accounting firm handpicked him when he completed his MBA with honors. Clearly, his was a charmed life.

Of course, James worked long hours since he didn't expect to get to the top without sacrifice. He enjoyed flaunting his possessions among his peers: a waterfront home, a company Mercedes, skiing in Aspen, diving in the Maldives. He and his wife, Helen, were familiar faces at the most fashionable restaurants in town. There was nothing James would deny Helen; she deserved to be pampered for quietly putting up with his workaholic ways.

Money was never a problem for the couple. But each year's end sparked a frenetic burst of spending on schemes to minimize taxes, all without regard to long-term goals or investment quality. Given James's position, banks cheerfully bankrolled his excesses.

Then one day, without warning, James's world collapsed like a row of dominoes. His investments plummeted in value, his debts mounted to uncontrollable proportions, and the IRS pursued him for unpaid taxes. Incredibly, he was declared bankrupt. Having become a liability to his firm's reputation, James was fired.

At fifty years of age, James was back to square one. He was unemployed, with nothing to show for his long hours of hard work and a lifetime of flashy success. By failing to plan, James let a series of ad hoc, incoherent decisions ultimately determine his long-term lifestyle. As the saying goes, James didn't plan to fail, he simply failed to plan.

It's seductive to believe that you're invincible when everything in your life appears to underscore that belief. Like the Kemptons, James Morley adopted the same approach to investment as he did to life—at his peril. He lost his sense of perspective and failed to answer the fundamental question "How much is enough?"

The Astute Dolphin

Warren Buffett, arguably the most successful investor of all time, started humbly. He bought his first stock for $38 at the ripe old age of eleven. Today in his late seventies, he is one of the world's richest men, worth close to $50 billion.

We assume Buffett knows something the rest of us don't. Yet his approach to investing is absurdly simple and old-fashioned. Resolutely ignoring Wall Street's fads and trends, his list of major share holdings reads like a dull shopping list: Coca-Cola, American Express, Gillette . . . not one Internet stock. There's nothing too exotic, just like the man himself.

He invests for the long term. Once he has thoroughly scrutinized a stock's inherent quality, prospects, and true value, he buys and holds it, patiently tolerant of ups and downs along the way. He draws on the philosopher Bertrand Russell's observation: "Most men would rather die than think. Many do." By contrast, Buffett emphasizes the importance of mastering his mind and hence his emotions.

Speaking with a Midwestern drawl, he points out that "to invest successfully during a lifetime does not require a stratospheric IQ, unusual business insights, or inside information. What's needed is a sound intellectual framework for making decisions and the ability to keep emotions from corroding that framework."

Buffett likes certainty. He believes "it's better to be sure of a good result than hopeful of a great one." Sound pedestrian? Consider this: Had you put $10,000 into Buffett's company in 1965, you'd have more than $50 million today, 100 times more than if you'd invested in Wall Street's S&P 500 Index.

Although Buffett has done better than any of us can ever dream to, his basic investment approach is available to all: Study the quality and value of stocks, set long-term goals, and develop a plan and stick to it.

Characteristic of his discipline and rationality, at the peak of the financial panic of 2008, Buffett wrote the following in the *New York Times*: "I haven't the faintest idea as to whether stocks will be higher or lower a month—or a year—from now. What is likely, however, is that the market will move higher, perhaps substantially so, well before either sentiment or the economy turns up." Not surprisingly, Buffett has been a calm and substantial buyer of shares in the midst of the financial crisis, laying the foundations for the next phase of growth in the wealth of his shareholders.

HOW MUCH IS ENOUGH?

This book explores the key behaviors that contribute to happiness in life and financial success. It will show you how to become wealthier and more fulfilled. And it will help you to follow your own path—encompassing your own values, goals, and financial and investment strategies—and overcome the psychological limitations of the brain. You will learn about the types of behavior that lead to success—and those to avoid—as well as how to ensure that your wealth-creation strategy is closely aligned with your values and goals, rather than being driven by forces such as peer pressure and consumerism.

We draw on new and emerging research on the complex links between wealth and happiness. We refer to work in economics, finance, behavioral finance, psychology, and philosophy. At the end of parts 1 and 2, we provide you with a range of resources that explore in greater depth the issues of wealth management on the one hand and meaning in life on the other.

Our experience of working with financial advisers and their clients around the world during the past twenty-five years adds an important practical element to this research. Generally speaking, we have observed that those people who have the greatest sense of fulfilment are also best at adopting sensible, focused investment strategies.

How Much Is Enough? is one of the first attempts to integrate this rich and diverse array of information into a single coherent and practical guide. Parts of the book will appeal to the rational, thinking mind and parts to your emotional side. Achiving both wealth and well-being requires you to combine both in a balanced way.

The book is divided into three parts. Part 1, The Bridge of Well-being, looks at how to define and understand your values and goals, how to achieve personal well-being, and how to teach your children about money and happiness.

Chapter 1 provides an overview of how to build your Bridge of Well-being, explaining each of the three key pillars for success. Chapter 2 shows how peer pressure, groupthink, and materialism often cause us to lose perspective on what's really important, and what to do about it. Chapter 3 looks at insights from some of the leading researchers on happiness, the way the mind works, and how we can capture the Happiness Prize. Chapter 4 outlines a range of simple, proven strategies for well-being, which can be acted on immediately. Chapter 5 suggests a framework for helping your kids make good choices about the role of money and happiness in their lives. Chapter 6 explores the opportunity to go one step further and achieve a meaningful life that involves using your strengths to make a difference in the lives of others.

Part 2, Wealth Habits, is all about the behavior that contributes to wealth. It focuses on practical ways to enhance your wealth and to overcome the "thought traps" that prevent this. Chapter 7 explains why shares have produced higher returns than other investments over long periods; why the average investor has missed out; and what you can do to capture the Investment Prize. Chapter 8 describes our emotional reactions to the rises and falls in markets and how to manage your responses in order to achieve success. Chapter 9 discusses the futility of a short-term approach to investment and suggests practical, prudent strategies to overcome this. Chapter 10 looks at why residential property investors behave differently from share investors and explains why an excessive focus on property is a common expensive obstacle to wealth. Chapter 11 helps you understand irrational ideas that can distract you from the important business of long-term wealth creation and teaches you how to counteract them.

Part 3, Wealth and Well-being, reviews the role of professional advice and discusses how wealth creation strategy contributes directly to well-being. Chapter 12 tells you how to find an effective financial adviser and coach and provides a case study that demonstrates how a good plan can make a big difference in one's life. Chapter 13 draws together the main themes of the book, which aim to help you capture the Ultimate Prize: the right relationship between money and happiness. It further helps you to answer for yourself the million-dollar question "How much is enough?" For what is money without happiness? What is wealth without well-being? And what is life without meaning?

One final note. To get the most out of reading *How Much Is Enough?* pause for a minute or two to consider the Reflections that you will find at the end of key sections of the book. These simple prompts will encourage you to think about a particular aspect of your life or money habits and consider what you might do differently. Acting on them will help you turn awareness into real and lasting change.

Part 1

THE BRIDGE OF WELL-BEING:

Understanding what's important to you and how to achieve it

Chapter 1

THE FOUNDATIONS

ELIZABETH AND SEBASTIAN WORTHINGTON WERE IN THEIR TWENTIES when they got married; she was a teacher and he a senior bank executive. Life was comfortable and luxuries affordable—even in London, one of the world's most expensive cities. After a few years they bought a semide-tached house with the thought of raising a family in mind.

By their midthirties, the couple had four boys under the age of six. Now they were reliant on Sebastian's salary alone and faced the classic prob-lems of the single-income professional family. Although his earnings had increased, so had the young father's responsibilities and working hours.

Elizabeth loved being a stay-at-home mother, but the layout of their house caused problems. The small kitchen was separate from the living area, and the stove was within easy reach of small hands.

Feeling guilty about working long hours, Sebastian suggested they renovate by adding an extra bedroom and creating an open-plan, family-friendly living area. It would take time to save the £50,000 they needed, but it would be worth it.

Sebastian's friends at work proposed a much quicker solution than sav-ing. With London property booming, the couple could simply borrow a small deposit for an apartment that was due to be constructed and sell it two or three years later, just before completion, for a handsome profit. His friends claimed that Sebastian and his wife would make much more than they would need to cover the costs of renovating their house—and there would be no capital outlay.

Elizabeth and Sebastian, dreaming of how the renovation would change their lives, were vulnerable. They were beginning to realize that they'd never gain serious wealth even though they were professionals. A wonderful opportunity now seemed to present itself. What, after all, could go wrong with bricks and mortar?

Not long after they borrowed the deposit for the apartment, London real estate went into a tailspin. Seeing stormy times ahead, the developer sped up construction and moved the completion date forward a whole year. The very week that Elizabeth and Sebastian started to get renovation quotes, they received a settlement demand. So bad was the slump by that time that the developer was releasing other apartments in the complex at a discount. The equation was ugly: a loss of £50,000 if the couple sold, or a deposit of £50,000 to settle, which meant the prospect of servicing a large loan—for years.

The stress put their marriage under tremendous strain and took the harried wife and mother to the verge of a breakdown.

MAKING THE RIGHT CHOICES

The Worthingtons' story, based on a real family, is far from unusual. The good news is that there are a number of easy-to-follow strategies you can use to avoid the traps they experienced and get ahead. This chapter explains these strategies and how you can apply them to develop a personal financial framework that will help guide you through life.

We call this framework our *Bridge of Well-being*. Three pillars underpin it.

1. Define and understand your values and goals.

2. Apply your resources to achieve your goals.

3. Develop your investment strategy.

A sound financial strategy is an important part of enjoying the life you choose to live; investments are an essential part of most financial strategies.

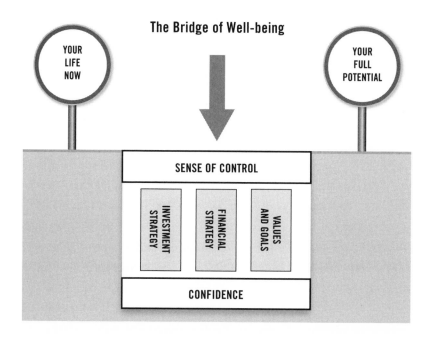

The Bridge of Well-being

The journey to wealth and well-being is always a work in progress. We should be grateful for this. Life would become pretty dull if one day we woke up and had achieved everything we were capable of accomplishing!

REFLECTIONS: How strong are your "three pillars"? If you have a partner, would he or she give the same answers you gave?

BUILDING YOUR BRIDGE OF WELL-BEING

Lifestyle financial planning focuses on more than simply having more money and possessions than the next person. It involves looking inward to uncover your values and goals, then making choices that are consistent with them rather than treating money as a measure of success. Too few people use plans that reflect what they really hope to achieve in life. You need to develop a financial plan for yourself—*not for your money.*

Different values and goals require varied financial strategies and investment approaches. For example, decisions about how much investment risk to take will differ between a couple who are caring for a child with a disability and a couple who are DINKS (that is, double income no kids) who vacation at luxury resorts and buy a new car every other year. The aim of lifestyle financial planning is to help you experience the good life you want to live, knowing sufficient money is there to support you.

As we will explore in the coming chapters, beyond a basic level of wealth, researchers can find no direct link between happiness and a high income or a large bank balance. Buying a Mercedes instead of a Lexus, or a $300 pair of shoes instead of some that cost $100, is not enough to make us happy.

Research conducted by ipac securities found there was only one essential factor separating people who rated themselves as highly satisfied with their lives from those who felt vulnerable. This was a sense of feeling in control of their financial situation. It applied whether the individual was making a six-figure salary or was earmarking each paycheck to cover the basic necessities of life.

Those who rated themselves highly satisfied had a financial plan. It wasn't necessarily detailed. Some were as simple as doing a monthly budget or setting basic saving goals. Some weren't even written down, but they were plans nonetheless.

Clinical psychologist Timothy Sharp, author of *The Happiness Handbook* and founder and "chief happiness officer" of The Happiness Institute, says that financial goals are part of a much bigger goal-setting program. "Truly content people are in control of several key domains of their lives—work, health, recreation, social life, money, and relationships—and they aim to balance their time and effort across them."

REFLECTIONS: Do you feel completely in control of your financial situation now? Do you have a clear financial strategy you are working toward, and is this built specifically to support the life you want to live?

Pillar 1: Define and Understand Your Values and Goals

The starting point is to be clear about your values and goals, which should be consistent with what is important in your life.

Easier said than done? If we all knew exactly what makes us happy, we could do it all the time, couldn't we? That's part of our problem, according to Dr. Sharp. We spend too little time thinking about what would make us happy and disproportionate amounts of time and effort chasing goals that don't bring the satisfaction we seek.

Stephanie Dowrick, author of *Choosing Happiness,* writes that values can support you when they shift the way you see a situation and respond to it. While it's easy enough to be attracted to noble values such as goodness, kindness, and freedom, the real question is what drives our choices when it comes to the issue of how and where we spend our time, energy, and money.

Later on we explore some ways to determine what's important and what is not. At this point in the discussion, it's important to sort your goals into the following time frames as you think through them:

- **Short-term, immediate goals** relating to what makes your life pleasurable right now. These could include going out weekly to a restaurant, a monthly getaway with your partner, vacations, or attending professional development workshops to improve your chances of career advancement.

- **Medium-term goals** relating to the foreseeable future. These could include acquiring your first house or upgrading the existing one, having a family, educating children, or taking a lengthy vacation abroad.

- **Longer-term goals** relating to when you want to retire, and what your lifestyle will be then. Often you will find that these will be extensions of your medium-term goals.

When setting goals, look forward, not back. This is harder than it sounds, since it goes against our natural inclinations. Too often, people look back at what they've learned, at what qualifications they've achieved, and at what loved ones have identified as their strengths and weaknesses.

The problem with this approach is that your future is dictated by the limitations of your past. As the saying goes, "If you do what you've always done, you'll get what you've always got." Many times we let limiting beliefs get in the way.

While others may be concerned about the possibility of your failing and getting hurt, you are the only one who knows what you really want—and what risks and challenges you're prepared to take to achieve it.

So suspend reality and the limitations of the past and think about what makes you energized and excited about living.

REFLECTIONS: If you had the chance to write the eulogy to be given at your own funeral, what would you like to say you had achieved? If someone were to describe you to a person who had never met you, how would you like to be described?

In *The Happiness Handbook*, Sharp suggests some simple but powerful exercises to jump-start people's thinking about their personal goals. With his permission, we have included them here for you to practice.

Exercise 1. Visualize yourself in five, ten, or twenty years. Start with twenty years hence. Your life is great; you're really happy. What does that life look like? Now step back to ten years. What are you doing to build toward that great life? How will you plan to achieve those goals? Go back again and repeat this process until you've broken your ideal life into more accessible chunks. At the end of the process you should have an achievable plan. You can then start taking real steps to achieve the life you want.

Exercise 2. Think more often about the changes you need to make to become happier. On a sheet of paper, make two columns and label them Problems and Benefits. In the Problems column, write down as many things as you can think of that you feel will prevent you from making these changes. In the Benefits column, list as many benefits as you can think of that will happen if and when you change. Now go back to the Problems column. Can you easily surmount these obstacles, or do they present major challenges? If they do, rephrase the problem in such a way that you can actually transfer the difficulty to the Benefits column.

For example, one problem you might list is the time required to make the changes. Your schedule during the coming week is the usual juggle of work, family, and social activities—all drawing you in different directions. But maybe the reason that you feel "time poor" is because you have not, in fact, taken the time to plan. One of the benefits of making the changes may well be that they free up time for you to focus on what's important, rather than what's urgent. It's all in the way you look at the problem.

These exercises help you think about what actions you need to take to make changes and realistically assess perceived obstacles.

EXPLORING YOUR GOALS   Here are some questions that we and other leading financial advisers use to help clients explore their goals. Take a few moments to think through your own answer to each question.

- What is your biggest achievement, and why?
- What is your greatest fear in relation to your future?
- What motivates you?
- What causes you stress?
- If you had unlimited means, what's the one thing you would like to do with your time that you are not doing today?
- What is the one personal goal you would like to achieve within the next year? What about three to five years?
- Where do you want to be in five to ten years time, professionally, personally, and financially?
- What is the state of your relationship with your partner, and what do you imagine it will be like in five years' time? What can you do to improve it?
- What are your hobbies? What do you like to buy with your spare money?

- Is there a legacy you would like to leave in your business life? In your personal life? In your family relationships?

- What are the most important things that you and your family want to achieve in the future? How would you feel if you couldn't achieve them? What are you prepared to give up now to achieve them?

- How much money is enough? Why? And how do you know?

In chapters 2 to 5, we look with more depth at ways to identify what is most important to you and strategies to achieve a greater sense of well-being—to capture what we call the Happiness Prize. At this juncture, however, it is worthwhile starting with the question "How much is enough for retirement?" as you begin to define and understand your values and goals.

One aspect of determining how much money is enough is planning for security in retirement. Here is a simple rule of thumb to help you estimate the amount of money that may be required.

Once work stops, the young adult children eventually leave home, and expenses decline, most people find that they need around 75 percent of their final working income to sustain a good lifestyle in retirement. (This assumes that the mortgage is paid off and there are no major debts outstanding.) Some people want more, of course, and many get by on much less, but 75 percent is usually a comfortable amount.

To work out how much money you'll need to retire on, simply start with the salary you expect to be earning immediately before you stop work. While we use U.S. dollars in the examples below, you can convert and substitute your own country's currency, whether it is Euros, pounds, rupees, and so forth.

> For males:
> To retire at age 50, multiply your final salary by 11.
> To retire at age 55, multiply your final salary by 10.
> To retire at age 60, multiply your final salary by 9.
> To retire at age 65, multiply your final salary by 8.
> To retire at age 70, multiply your final salary by 7.

How Much Is Enough? Retirement Calculator (Male)

Your desired retirement age	Salary before you stop work	Multiplied by	Lump sum required
50	$50,000	11	$550,000
	$100,000		$1,100,000
	$150,000		$1,650,000
55	$50,000	10	$500,000
	$100,000		$1,000,000
	$150,000		$1,500,000
60	$50,000	9	$450,000
	$100,000		$900,000
	$150,000		$1,350,000
65	$50,000	8	$400,000
	$100,000		$800,000
	$150,000		$1,200,000
70	$50,000	7	$350,000
	$100,000		$700,000
	$150,000		$1,050,000

These numbers are only a rough guide, particularly because they assume the average life expectancy and that all capital is exhausted during your lifetime. If you live for longer than the average, then you will run out of money. Please also note that we have ignored the effects of taxation and U.S. Social Security benefits.

The "How Much Is Enough? Retirement Calculator" we've created provides an estimate of lump sum amounts required for retirement at various ages, using the multiples outlined above. Everyone is different, so the amount you need may differ from the numbers shown. Nevertheless, it provides a useful benchmark.

Our calculator assumes that the required retirement income is 75 percent of final salary and that investments earn a return (after taking inflation into account) of 5 percent annually. If you were to earn a real (after inflation) investment return of 0 rather than 5 percent, however, the effect on the lump sum required would be significant. For example, a male who wishes to retire at age 60 would need a lump sum of 16 times his final salary rather than 9 times if he failed to capture this return—a huge difference.

This reflects the power of compounding over a long period of time. The good news, as we explore in part 2, is that it is within the power of most of us to capture the Investment Prize (which we describe later in this chapter under the heading "Pillar 3: Develop Your Investment Strategy"), which provides a good chance of earning a real return of 5 percent per annum over the longer term.

Females usually require more for retirement because they enjoy a longer life expectancy. For example, on average a 45-year-old female today can expect to live approximately 5 years longer than her male counterpart.

> For females:
> To retire at age 50, multiply your final salary by 12.
> To retire at age 55, multiply your final salary by 11.
> To retire at age 60, multiply your final salary by 10.
> To retire at age 65, multiply your final salary by 9.
> To retire at age 70, multiply your final salary by 8.

To estimate how much money you'll need and to see the impact of varying such factors as your expected retirement age, visit our website at www. howmuchisenough.net and use our proprietary retirement calculator. This easy-to-use tool enables you to specify a number of variables, including gender, desired age of retirement, current salary, proportion of current salary required in retirement, and the level of investment return expected.

Once you have determined your goals, you may find that you have such a long list that you can't possibly achieve them all. If so, then it's time to make some choices. None of us can have everything we want, so we need to *prioritize*. We have to choose between money spent today on short-term goals such as leisure activities and money saved for the long term so that we could, for example, retire earlier. In chapter 4 you'll find valuable

How Much Is Enough? Retirement Calculator (Female)

Your desired retirement age	Salary before you stop work	Multiplied by	Lump sum required
50	$50,000	12	$600,000
	$100,000		$1,200,000
	$150,000		$1,800,000
55	$50,000	11	$550,000
	$100,000		$1,100,000
	$150,000		$1,650,000
60	$50,000	10	$500,000
	$100,000		$1,000,000
	$150,000		$1,500,000
65	$50,000	9	$450,000
	$100,000		$900,000
	$150,000		$1,350,000
70	$50,000	8	$400,000
	$100,000		$800,000
	$150,000		$1,200,000

ideas to help you choose what's of most importance to you. At this point, however, you should concentrate on the second pillar in your Bridge of Well-being.

REFLECTIONS: If you're approaching retirement, how does your financial position stack up? Have you defined what a "good retirement" looks like? Do you need to or can you afford to wait?

Pillar 2: Apply Your Resources to Achieve Your Goals

Once we define our goals, we can work back to the present and consider what's required to achieve them.

Begin by mapping out your financial resources today and what will be available in the future. This is easier to do—and more fun—than it sounds. In fact, if you have spent time thinking about what you want to achieve at various stages of your life, this exercise can be very enlightening.

There are four basic steps to follow in learning how to apply your resources to achieve your goals. First, identify your current income and expenditures by doing a budget. Don't be too precise; estimates will get you started. You can get a budget planner from any office supply store, or ask a financial adviser to suggest one. Also list your assets and liabilities to work out your estimated net wealth.

Second, estimate your income and expenditures in the medium term (three years) and longer term (five to ten years). Taking into account your savings potential, estimate the growth in your assets (net of liabilities) in the medium term, at the point of retirement, and a couple of years into retirement. It's a valuable exercise to calculate how long your estimated retirement savings will last, given your desired lifestyle.

Third, balance your current and future needs and goals. As you go through this process, you will start to see how many of the goals that are important to you are affordable, given your current plans. One of the biggest challenges that we face is reconciling our strong desire for security and a good lifestyle in retirement with the many pressing day-to-day demands—particularly if we have teenagers or aging parents.

This is a great problem in parts of the United States and Asia, where cultural expectations are that aged parents will be supported by their off-spring, for longer and more expensive retirements than ever before. At the same time, the costs of raising and educating children are rising steeply. Plus, most working adults want to have a life for themselves as well, rather than purely supporting the needs of their families. Not surprisingly, such middle-agers refer to themselves as the "sandwich generation."

Fourth, treat savings and investment as complementary. Often, too much emphasis is put on investment returns and not enough on savings. Savings can be thought of as the cake; investing savings to enhance their value over time is the icing. The first step to happiness is spending less than you earn. This is why investing in property historically has been so benefi-cial for millions of people even though the long-term return on housing is not high (as we explain in detail in chapter 10). A significant debt burden in the form of a mortgage forces savings like no other investment, provided that—as the sub-prime crisis that started in 2007 highlighted—one can afford the mortgage repayments.

If you save a dollar, it doesn't make much difference to your wealth if the return after one year is plus-5 percent or minus-5 percent. But you have nothing at all if you don't save the dollar in the first place. Over time, investment returns can compound massively. Combined with a regular savings plan, this means the cake will grow very large and the icing very thick. So, once you have completed your budget, determine your surplus and make sure you *lock it away each month* in a regular savings plan.

REFLECTIONS: Think about where your lazy money goes. Are there any areas you could cut back on without sacrificing your lifestyle? How often do you wear most of the clothes you buy? Should you take the occasional taxi and sell the second car? This alone could save you thousands of dollars a year. Where are the hollow logs in your household budget?

BECOME SMART ABOUT SAVING　Recognizing the difficulty many people have with saving money, economics professors Richard Thaler and Shlomo Benartzi devised a special savings plan called the Saving More Tomorrow Plan (SmarT Plan). If you have difficulty with saving, it's worth trying to access this plan, which is now offered in many countries and through various pension plans. The SmarT Plan is based on the following behavioral decision-making insights:

- Many people want to save more, but they lack self-control.
- Self-control restrictions are easier to accept if they take effect in the future.
- Investors are very sensitive to perceived losses.
- People procrastinate about making changes to their savings plans.

In order to counteract those behaviors, the SmarT Plan has been constructed to achieve the following.

- Savings increases are synchronized with salary increases.
- People are precommitted to saving more—but only in the future.
- People remain in the plan unless they actively drop out.

In one instance where the SmarT Plan was introduced to an American pension-plan environment, the participation rate increased by 25 percent among employees, and after just three years, the savings rate among participants was double that of employees who were not part of the plan.

The main reasons for the SmarT Plan's effectiveness were the elements of precommitment, automation, and the default settings, meaning that more thought and action were required to get out of the plan than to stick with it.

CLOSE THE GAP BETWEEN YOUR FINANCIAL RESOURCES AND YOUR GOALS   Matching your financial resources to your identified goals is not always simple. There may well be a gap between your goals and your financial ability to achieve them. Taking greater investment risks is one way to help close that gap, but it is not a panacea. You may also need to make choices about which goals are most important and how much you are prepared to risk in order to achieve them. You may find there are goals you wish to forget. Others you may want to pursue with renewed vigor.

For example, in order to buy a second house at the beach and spend more quality time with your family, you may choose to invest in a high-growth portfolio for a long period. Compared with investing in a more secure but low-return portfolio, this will increase your chances of affording the beach house over time. It may also put at risk your plans to expand the house in which you now live. To meet this challenge, you might decide to seek a promotion at work, or simply save harder. To make the right choices, you need to understand all the probable outcomes of different scenarios. That will lead you to create the third pillar of your Bridge of Well-being.

Pillar 3: Develop Your Investment Strategy

After you have identified your goals and mapped out your financial resources, you will need to address the final element of your personal financial framework, which is to develop an investment strategy.

One of the most important investment decisions you will make is to determine what exposure to such growth assets as shares and property you need in your portfolio to give you the best chance of achieving your goals, taking into account your present and expected future financial position. This will help you determine how much investment risk is appropriate, based on real issues and choices rather than an arbitrary assessment taken from a questionnaire that categorizes you somewhere between "aggressive risk taker" and "risk averse."

To do this, you need to see beyond the substantial short-term volatility in investment markets and have a realistic understanding of the returns available in the long term. Analysis of the experience of the major market economies suggests that the major asset classes are likely to produce the following real (after inflation) returns in the long run:

Cash: 0–1 percent
Bonds: 1–3 percent
Property: 3–5 percent
Shares: 5–8 percent

The most important point to note is the long-term superior return produced by a diversified portfolio of shares—what we call the Investment Prize, and loosely defined as an additional amount of money that will make a big difference to funding your lifestyle and retirement needs. In chapters 7 through 9 we examine the reasons for the Investment Prize and how to capture it in more detail.

(Note that strategies such as gearing, or borrowing to invest, can be used to increase your portfolio's expected return significantly, but they also increase its risk. Likewise, higher returns than the long-term ones shown above are achievable, but they generally involve speculation, or gambling, or they occur over such a short time frame as to be a meaningless guide.)

Although there are literally hundreds of books and manuals on investment strategies, you don't need to embark on a long reading program to be a successful investor. All you need is a basic understanding of the Four Golden Principles—Quality, Value, Diversity, and Time—and good advice.

Investing in a Quality investment at a price that represents good Value in a Diverse range and for sufficient Time will bring you the rewards you seek. We explore the Four Golden Principles in much more detail in chapter 11.

Even if all you do is simply capture the returns from markets, the power of compound interest means that during the long term it's going to make a big difference to what you can achieve. The trick is to do what so few people seem able to manage: stay the course with a sensibly diversified portfolio.

Now that you have explored the foundations of your Bridge of Well-being, you are ready to look at how you can put such a framework into place for yourself. You will also look at some of the challenges you will face.

If your financial strategy supports the achievement of what is most important to you, as opposed to simply the accumulation of possessions, your bridge will be much stronger and more resilient. You will enjoy the Ultimate Prize of a life rich in meaning and underpinned by financial confidence.

Chapter 2

THE MEANING OF MONEY

To begin defining and understanding your values, ask yourself these three questions: What does money mean to me? What is the role of money in my life? How much money is enough? These seem to be simple enough to ask and answer, but many people never take the time to consider them. Research shows that such questions often elicit a maze of emotions. Understanding the meaning of money in our lives, and these emotions, will help us become both wealthier and happier.

We all know someone who appears to have it all—except for genuine happiness and contentment. And most of us also know someone who has few possessions, yet leads a fulfilling life. Do the following couples sound familiar?

Roger and Heather live in a California-style bungalow with ocean views. The couple had taken out a modest mortgage to move to their larger bungalow when their second child was born. Roger's annual bonus is the equivalent of an average person's salary and, by anyone's standards, the couple could be considered very well off. Everything about their lifestyle other than the affluent neighborhood they live in, however, suggests a struggle to make ends meet.

In an apparent attempt to achieve ever-greater financial security, the family has gone without many basic pleasures. They drive an old but reliable yellow Volvo dotted with patches of rust, wear frayed clothes, buy the cheapest cuts of meat, and use a set of hair clippers to avoid the cost of a decent haircut. Their house is crammed with possessions that Roger says "might come in handy one day." The money they save goes straight into their pension fund, which, thanks to their sacrifice, has already accumulated more than $600,000, despite the couple still being in their thirties.

Jim and Simone, their neighbors, welcomed Roger and Heather when they moved in, but recently they've given up inviting the couple over to enjoy lounging by their backyard pool and hot tub. For a start, Roger and Heather never brought a decent bottle of wine with them. Then they always wanted to talk about council rates, taxes, and how little you could live on "if you really tried."

Despite their huge mortgage, Jim and Simone are not about to deny themselves any of life's pleasures. They've worked hard and deserve them. Jim had always wanted a convertible sports car, and now he has one. Simone has a penchant for fine champagne—"the cheap stuff irritates my nose," she says—and collects exquisite Japanese etchings.

Since they are self-employed, Jim and Simone do not have pension plans. Simone thinks the government is "mad to think they can tell me how to spend my money," and Jim agrees that life is for living and long-term savings are strictly for conservatives. In their quieter moments, though, both have a slightly uneasy sense that the life they are enjoying is built on shaky foundations.

While these couples are at opposite ends of the spectrum of attitudes toward money, it is clear that their lifestyles arise from more than simple decisions on whether or not to spend. Deep-seated psychological factors and often hidden emotions are usually behind people's money behavior. Psychotherapist Stephen Jenkinson argues that money arouses "prehistoric" desires for safety, security, and plenty, plus anxieties it cannot hope to satisfy.

Furthermore, psychologist Valerie Wilson has found that the four words most associated with money are all negative: *anxiety, depression, anger,* and *helplessness*. She says that while television programs about the rich and famous may help fuel our desires for the good life, most of us appear to be driven not by greed, but by fear.

Roger and Heather may be afraid of their ability to cope should they ever strike financial hardship, even though rational analysis would say their future looks very secure indeed. Jim and Simone may fear losing their friends and self-esteem if forced to live within their means.

REFLECTIONS: Are you more like the conservative Roger and Heather, or more like Jim and Simone, who are extravagant with money?

WHO'S TEACHING YOUR CHILDREN ABOUT MONEY?

Money elicits an incredible range of emotions and behaviors, from greed, pain, and arrogance to jealousy, betrayal, and sheer lust—and more. All this turmoil makes a joke of the traditional economist's definition of money as a "neutral medium of exchange." In fact, Dr. Wilson puts it well when she argues that money is as much emotional as legal tender.

She believes that troubled relationships with money usually stem from childhood. Research consistently shows that money habits are generally inculcated before a child's tenth birthday. Yet few parents talk freely with their children about money. And through lack of communication, or by their actions, many parents fail to help their children understand the role that money should play in their lives. Specifically, they misunderstand how money relates to their values, their achievements, their goals, and their overall well-being.

Consequently, money assumes a strange mystique. Further, because of the unexplored area of money and personal values, it is often seen as a measure of personal worth rather than simply an enabler.

Ask yourself these questions:

- Did my parents freely answer my childhood questions about how much money they earned?

- Did they guide me through the broader role money can play in life, either through words or actions?

- How comfortable would I feel answering my children's questions about my salary and use of money?

- What if my earnings and money behavior became a topic of conversation at a dinner party? Would I feel uncomfortable? Why?

Surprisingly, Wilson's research shows that most people feel more comfortable talking to their children about sex than about money. This is poor preparation for children in an era of complex choices and enormous pressure to spend rather than to save. Those who don't understand the meaning of money are poorly equipped to deal with an ever-more-complex world. Like sex, money is something most of us deal with every day, and we had better be prepared.

REFLECTIONS: Think about your answers to the preceding list of questions. What emotional baggage do you carry from your past with respect to money? Did your parents use money as a device to control your behavior? Was your pocket money inadequate? Did you feel like the poor kid on the block? As a first step toward understanding your money behavior today, it's worth identifying ways in which money may have played a role in shaping your development.

We will explore the fascinating world of kids, money, and happiness in chapter 5, but for now, if you are the parent of young children, start planning your next conversation about what money really means to you, your family, and to them. If you can find the words to explain this to your children, you should be well on the way to understanding this fully for yourself. You will also be one step closer to answering the question, "How much is enough?"

Eileen's Story

The O'Reillys' relationship with their daughter, Eileen, had become troubled. Shortly after starting at her exclusive new private school at age thirteen, Eileen had become body-conscious and started experimenting with diets. She also began demanding money to buy clothes that her parents considered faddish, skimpy, and expensive.

Eileen's dieting became obsessive. Her once-excellent school reports now contained notes about her disruptive influence on her classmates.

Increasingly, she found fault with her parents, whom she seemed to regard as embarrassing losers.

They still remember with anguish the afternoon she returned home from school demanding the latest cell phone. All the kids had one, she had said. The O'Reillys had always wanted their four children to learn the value of thrift, so they had resisted this demand.

Eileen's obstinacy and sullenness worsened. Eventually, her parents tried to bring in professional help, but Eileen was evasive. She wouldn't turn up for counseling sessions. Worried and unsure what to do, Sean O'Reilly finally bought her what he considered an adequate phone. He was shocked by his daughter's vitriolic response, especially when she accused him of "completely ruining [her] life."

The O'Reillys' daughter had become like a stranger to them—an insecure, belligerent, and avaricious teenager.

Following Eileen's death three years later as a result of complications associated with her eating disorder, the O'Reillys learned of the torment she had suffered from prolonged bullying at school. They read in the diary Eileen had kept that Sinead O'Sullivan, a striking blonde, had led the "in crowd" in their verbal attacks on Eileen. The teens all stayed in touch through constant text-messaging. Eileen could not join in. The other girls also teased her unmercifully about her clothes, her looks, and her neighborhood.

The impact of such petty bullying might seem hard to appreciate until we remember how sensitive we ourselves were as young people, and how much we desired acceptance. Most teenagers see the world almost entirely through the eyes of their peers; their parents' opinions are a poor second. Adolescents and teens are also particularly vulnerable to images in the media about what constitutes the perfect body and what possessions are "must-haves." Advertisers are not in the business of encouraging contemplation of how much is enough; their motto is "the more the better."

Child psychologist Michael Carr-Gregg has powerfully dealt with the vicious nature of bullying in girls' schools in his book *The Princess Bitchface Syndrome*. But such behavior has much wider implications. Perhaps the greatest tragedy is that Eileen's demand for a cool new phone, clothes, and other material things did not represent rejection of her parents. It simply reflected her intense desire to be accepted into the club.

Eileen's story illustrates the potentially overwhelming power of peer groups, particularly when combined with bullying related to status within a group. It shows how our behavior is susceptible to being shaped by others' expectations rather than from within. It shows how sometimes we let others determine how much is enough for us, instead of taking the more difficult path of working it out for ourselves. In an increasing number of cases—across all socioeconomic levels and in all age groups—peer pressure can be an important risk factor in serious psychological illness.

Consume, or Be Consumed

Viewing money as a measure of personal worth, combined with peer pressure, can distort a person's values, behavior, and decisions. This can further lead to distress and illness. Teenage girls are among the most vulnerable groups. Millions of young women experience enormous pressure to conform to media images of models airbrushed to impossible perfection and are thus at significant risk for conditions such as anorexia nervosa and bulimia. Perhaps the best-known example is that of the late Princess Diana, who battled with eating disorders for much of her life.

A 2008 report published by the YWCA in the United States called *Beauty at Any Cost* found that *80 percent* of women were unhappy with their appearance. The report also quoted a study that indicates aggressive bullying among girls—based on issues such as physical attributes and social status—has been on the rise since the early 1990s. As the report puts it, if you're constantly made to feel inadequate, you're quite disabled in terms of being able to achieve in other areas of life—academic, social, and political.

The desire to be accepted by the crowd, and the pressure to conform to social norms and "keep up with the Joneses," affects all of us—not merely teenagers. Decisions about the way we live our lives are influenced to a huge extent by the expectations, prejudices, and behaviors of those around us.

There is a powerful reason for this, which stems from the way the human brain has evolved. Those who are accepted into the herd or crowd gain protection from their peers, so they are more likely to survive and pass on their genes.

In today's world, however, the results of worrying excessively about the Joneses can have the opposite effect. This is because decisions that are made to satisfy the expectations of others may be those least likely to satisfy us. Overcoming this legacy with changed behaviors is one of the most significant challenges of modern life.

Peer pressure, when misdirected, is arguably one of the greatest threats to living according to personal values, and one of the greatest obstacles to exploring who we really are and how to live a full, meaningful life.

The Extreme Effects of Groupthink

Studies have repeatedly shown that groupthink is one of the single most powerful drivers of human behavior. It has been used to explain mass atrocities in Nazi Germany, Rwanda, and Bosnia. It helps us understand why otherwise intelligent company directors have made the collective decisions that led to corporate disasters. It also helps explain why the rich are often unhappy. There is always someone better-off, they think.

In her book *Staying Sane in a Changing World*, international change agent and strategist Margot Cairnes describes "collusion" as the tendency of any group to cooperate at a subconscious level to maintain group and personal comfort.

The rules of collusion ensure that we don't ask embarrassing questions and that, instead, we conform to unstated group norms. Cairnes refers to a number of examples of how groupthink has led some of the most senior military, political, and business leaders to make disastrous decisions.

Underpinning groupthink is a Them-and-Us focus. There is a chief bully, or "mind guard," who pulls dissenters into line. It appears that the desire for group acceptance and the fear of ridicule can be greater than a person's fear of being involved in a catastrophe.

In the corporate world, collusion and peer pressure played a key role in the spectacular 2001 collapse of the large American energy trading company Enron. Its failure cost thousands of people their jobs, and those who held company stock lost some or all of their retirement savings.

Many Enron executives were aware of at least part of the complex web of transactions and accounting treatments that eventually caused the giant corporation to collapse. However, it appears that few—if any—

took action until after the company's fall and thus after the worst effects had been felt.

Writing in *Time* magazine shortly after Enron sought bankruptcy protection, journalist Michael Duffy described its fall as

> The most revealing sort of failure. It is a failure of the old-fashioned idea that auditors, directors, and stock analysts are supposed to put the interests of shareholders above their own thirst for fees. It is a failure of government . . . And it is a failure of character.

The personal and professional stigma and long-term effects of being a whistle-blower, even when right is on your side, can be severe enough to deter good people. A whistle-blower is by definition stepping outside the accepted norms of behavior of his or her group and knows he or she could fail to convince outsiders. Such a step takes immense courage.

Journalists Richard Lacayo and Amanda Ripley found through interviewing corporate whistle-blowers that "almost all" of them said they *would not repeat* their actions. If they hadn't been fired, they had been cornered, isolated, or made irrelevant in their work lives. Many had gone on to suffer from alcoholism or depression. If this is the price for standing out, no wonder so many people simply follow the crowd, living lives dictated by the expectations of their peer group.

REFLECTIONS: Think of a time when the impact of others' opinions forced you into agreeing to decisions with which you were not comfortable. Would you handle the situation differently today? If so, what would you do and how would it likely make you feel?

LIVING IN A MATERIAL WORLD

Enron bosses appear to have been driven by image, which made them less resilient to peer pressure than if they had been able to focus on such inner goals as achievement or empathy.

There are many psychological influences that can have a strong effect on our behavior—often subconsciously, and more than most of us realize. Why are magazines that feature celebrities such huge sellers around the world? Why do kids in Africa know—or care—who Madonna is? She herself has the answer. In one of her biggest hits, she sings that we are "living in a material world."

Richard Eckersley of Australian National University sums it up well when he observes that consumerism constantly seeks ways to "colonize our consciousness," and as consumerism spreads, the goal of marketing becomes not only to make us dissatisfied with what we have but also with who we are. In other words, it encourages us to put aside questions such as "How much is enough?" and focus on the blind accumulation of more, on the assumption that this will somehow make us happier. Consumerism both fosters and exploits "the restless, insatiable expectation that there has to be more to life."

While we don't think of marketing as a form of bullying, it nonetheless tries to make us feel inadequate, just as boys and girls who hector one another do. Mass marketing's tactics are usually subtler and are backed by huge budgets. The result is relentless bombardment by countless messages in every part of our daily lives.

Sociologist Eckersley tells us that big business in the United States spends *more than $1,000 billion a year* on marketing, about twice the sum Americans spend annually on all levels of education. Or, as one Tibetan monk remarked when first confronted with America's advertising culture, "They are trying to steal our minds." Little wonder that the task of feeling personally secure and having a clear sense of inner direction is challenging. Recall how Sir Isaac Newton lost a fortune in the South Sea Bubble. Intelligence was no defense against the immense pressure of watching others grow wealthier.

A combination of peer pressure, groupthink, and celebrity materialism makes us vulnerable to a range of emotions, especially greed and envy, which are closely interrelated. Experiencing greed or envy or both can directly lead not only to financial disasters but also to life disasters. What can certainly help us face the material world we live in is not simply intelligence, but a deeper insight into what makes us happy. The very next chapter asks us to uncover the sources of our happiness.

Chapter 3

THE HAPPINESS CHALLENGE

Surprisingly, we're not very good at predicting what will make us happy. During the past ten years there has been an explosion of research into human happiness, stemming from the realization that tremendous rises in personal wealth and consumption have not been accompanied by increased personal happiness. While wealth has risen exponentially in the last fifty years, happiness levels have barely changed. Many of us have learned to evaluate our well-being by looking outward, at what we can buy and own, instead of inward, at the kind of people we are. And it's simply not making us feel better.

The quest for material possessions can be likened to taking a drug. Once the latest hit wears off, an even bigger dose is required to get the same effect. People quickly become accustomed to what they have and demand more as their expectations rise. Once they achieve these higher expectations, they wish for more again. This has been called the "hedonic treadmill." Once you step on, it is very difficult to get off. If such a treadmill didn't exist, we would become happier and happier the more possessions we accumulated, but the evidence shows this is not happening.

We are also not very good at determining what leisure activities will make us happy. Watching television is the number one leisure activity in the world. In many cases, people spend more time in front of a TV set than they do talking to their family and friends. Yet when was the last time you clambered off the couch late at night after an evening of watching television feeling great about yourself and good about the world? While we think that television will be a satisfying form of relaxation, it rarely is.

As Harvard psychology professor Dan Gilbert observes, our brains have a unique ability that allows us to mentally transport ourselves into the future and then ask ourselves how it feels to be there. But the process is far from perfect because when we imagine the future, we fill in details that won't really come to pass and leave out details that will. "When we imagine future feelings, we find it impossible to ignore what we are feeling now and impossible to recognize how we will think about the things that happen later."

Researchers call the gap between what we predict about the future and what we ultimately experience "impact bias." Perhaps the classic example of impact bias is the lottery-winner syndrome. The main reason people buy lottery tickets is the dramatic lure of becoming rich overnight, and a winner's sudden wealth is seen as the gateway to instant happiness. Who wouldn't like to win a million dollars? Wouldn't all our problems be solved? Wouldn't life be much easier? More relaxed? Happier?

The reality is usually different. Researchers report that lottery winners do indeed experience initial euphoria, but this wears off remarkably quickly. Within weeks, life pretty much returns to normal.

In this chapter we review the insights that have been produced by some of the leading researchers on happiness and the way the mind works.

THE COST OF HAPPINESS AND HEDONIC ARBITRAGE

We've all got used to thinking about the cost of things in terms of money. While this is convenient shorthand, the danger is that we end up like Oscar Wilde's definition of a cynic: "someone who knows the price of everything and the value of nothing." How do we compare the merits of a job that pays us more than our current one but will not make us feel as satisfied? If fulfilment is the ultimate goal of life, then why shouldn't this be the currency that we use to make such important decisions?

Recognizing the limitations of measuring everything in terms of money, economists have come up with the useful concept of "opportunity cost," which measures cost in terms of the next best thing we have foregone. As the Dutch mathematician Daniel Bernoulli said as early as 1738, "The determination of the value of an item must not be based on its price, but rather on the utility it yields." In this spirit, we propose the concept of the "hedonic opportunity cost" (HOC), in which the measurement is happiness foregone. For example, we would think of the cost of a much more expensive car in terms of, say, the additional happiness that a family vacation abroad may have produced. Closely linked to the idea of the HOC is the idea of "hedonic arbitrage," which refers to the potential to increase happiness without any increase in spending or wealth. This is an idea that we have been exploring with one of the most creative thinkers on this topic, Professor Benartzi, and some of his colleagues in a collaborative piece of behavioral research.

Now, you may protest that happiness is not as easy to measure as money is. Aren't hedonistic pleasures quite intangible compared to cold hard cash? Perhaps, but happiness is about our feelings, our inner well-being, and so what can be more important than learning how to connect with these feelings and using this as a measure of our success in life? We are talking here about nothing less than the Happiness Prize—that is, the ability to increase our happiness without the need for more money.

The remaining chapters in part 1 do precisely that: provide you with the framework, the knowledge, and the tools to better understand happiness, to explore your inner self, and to put flesh on the ideas of the HOC and hedonic arbitrage so that you can apply them in your daily life and capture the Happiness Prize.

How Happy Are You?

Before we proceed, please take a few minutes to complete this brief questionnaire, provided by founder Tim Sharp and used by permission of The Happiness Institute. The questions are designed to provide an assessment of your current levels of happiness. Just circle the appropriate answers and use the scale at the end to tally results. (Further information and a range of useful resources are available at www.thehappinessinstitute.com.)

1. (a) I feel miserable almost all the time.
   (b) I often feel miserable.
   (c) I usually feel neutral.
   (d) I usually feel pretty good.
   (e) I feel great almost all the time.

2. (a) I find life to be boring all the time.
   (b) I'm pretty bored with most aspects of life.
   (c) I find life boring at times, but at other times it interests me.
   (d) I'm interested in most aspects of life.
   (e) I find life and living to be absolutely fascinating.

3. (a) I have no direction or life purpose.
   (b) I'm unsure about my life direction and purpose.
   (c) Sometimes I feel as if I know my life purpose.
   (d) I'm pretty clear about my life purpose and direction.
   (e) My life purpose and direction are crystal clear.

4. (a) I have no energy and feel tired almost all the time.
   (b) I often feel tired and lethargic.
   (c) I usually have enough energy to do what I need to do.
   (d) Most of the time I feel energetic and enthusiastic.
   (e) I'm bursting with energy and enthusiasm almost all the time.

5. (a) I'm extremely pessimistic about the future.
   (b) There are times when I feel pessimistic about the future.
   (c) I'm not sure about the future, one way or the other.
   (d) I'm pretty optimistic about the future.
   (e) I'm extremely optimistic and excited about the future.

6. (a) I don't have any close friends.
   (b) I have a few friends but none I consider really close.
   (c) I have a few good friends and family members
       with whom I'm close.

(d) I have quite a few good friends.

(e) I have lots of good friends and easily connect with everyone.

7. (a) I don't think I have any strengths at all.

(b) I'm not sure whether or not I have any strengths.

(c) I'm getting to know my strengths.

(d) I know my strengths and try to use them when I can.

(e) I know exactly what my strengths are and use them all the time.

8. (a) I never enjoy myself no matter what I'm doing.

(b) I find it difficult to enjoy life in the moment.

(c) I try to enjoy life as much as I can.

(d) I enjoy myself most of the time.

(e) I thoroughly enjoy every moment.

9. (a) I have absolutely nothing for which to be grateful.

(b) There's not much in my life for which I'm grateful.

(c) I'm grateful for a few things in my life.

(d) I have quite a few things in my life for which I'm grateful.

(e) I'm extremely grateful for many things in my life.

10. (a) I've accomplished nothing.

(b) I've not accomplished much in life.

(c) I've accomplished about as much as the average person.

(d) I've accomplished more in life than most people.

(e) I've accomplished a great deal more in life than most people.

Score each question from 1 to 5 where (a) equals 1 and (e) equals 5 (the maximum possible score, therefore, is 50).

If you scored 40 or above, you're doing extremely well. Keep up the great work.

If you scored 30 to 39, you're doing pretty well but might like to review the questions on which you scored 3 or below and consider how you might improve in these areas.

If you scored below 29, you could be much happier!

While there are few shortcuts to happiness, the insights in this chapter on some of the key influences on happiness should be valuable, even for those who scored well on the happiness questionnaire.

The Wealth–Happiness Map

Does what we've said mean that money has little bearing on happiness, or even that money actually causes unhappiness? It's not that simple.

Compelling research suggests that the pursuit of money simply to buy more and more, or to keep up with the Joneses, can make us unhappy. But at the same time, above a daily subsistence struggle, more money can also make a big difference in our quality of life.

Thus, the important question about money is more complex than "how much?" and is more closely related to "what for?"

The value of economic production per person, adjusted for inflation, has tripled in the United States since 1958. Economist Robert Shiller has calculated how this extra wealth has been spent. He found that 27 percent of this huge increase went to medical care, 23 percent to homes, 12 percent to transportation, 10 percent to recreation, 9 percent to personal business activities, and 8 percent to food. Clothing and personal care took just 3 and 1 percent, respectively, of the extra money. "Thus, most of the money was spent on staying healthy, having a nice home, traveling and relaxing, and doing a little business," writes Shiller.

Based on this breakdown, it is clear that more wealth does make a contribution to well-being. The real difference between the happy and unhappy rich is that the former see money as a means to an end, a contributor to the achievement of goals that are consistent with their personal values, rather than an end in itself. The unhappy rich are often those who pursue wealth without regard to well-being.

The ancient Greek philosopher Aristotle understood this. He viewed money as having two functions: as a means to an end, and as an end in itself. He felt the latter was fraught with peril. In other words, the pursuit of money for its own sake, with no connection to what is truly important to us, is unlikely to improve our lives. As a means to an end, however, it may be an altogether different story, as two of the world's richest people, Microsoft

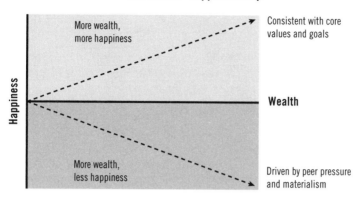

founder Bill Gates and investor Warren Buffett, have shown through their charitable work. Building substantial wealth can bring the great satisfaction of making a difference in the lives of others, as well as your own, and this is an important part of what constitutes a meaningful life.

The Wealth–Happiness Map shown above highlights the significant impact that your motivation for wanting to become wealthy has on whether or not more money actually makes you happier.

VALUES AND GOALS

An emerging body of research highlights the importance of personal values as a contributor to happiness, and it points to various factors that have a significant impact on our quality of life.

Understanding and living consistently with your personal values is one of the major pathways to happiness. Yet recent changes in society, in particular a focus on consumerism, can easily distract us from our deepest values and beliefs. It is easy to lose sight of just how much is enough.

Until relatively recently, thrift was considered a virtue. Saving for a rainy day was seen as sensible. Conspicuous consumption was vulgar. People planned for the future—and saved accordingly. The idea of being in debt was anathema; layaway—that is, waiting until you could afford an item—was preferred to credit. There was a certain social cachet in being able to

Shifts in Cultural Attitudes

From	To
Thrifty (positive connotation)	Tight (negative connotation)
Save for a rainy day	Buy a home theater for rainy days
Extravagance/indulgence	Lifestyle
Plan for the future	Live for the day
Debt is "bad"	Credit is "good"
Wait until I can afford it	Have it now

say that you had saved for the future and had insurance against the possible financial impact of disaster.

Banks were pivotal in educating people about the virtues of saving, and cautious in providing credit. They encouraged the rapid repayment of debt.

In a single generation, these values have been reversed.

Instant gratification is now encouraged and has become the norm. Underpinning the subprime disaster that rocked financial markets in 2007–2008 is the fact that banks have become major boosters of a credit and consumption boom, through issuing credit cards (what we call plastic money), mortgages, unsecured loans, or equity-release products such as reverse mortgages. Banks now like us to be in their debt, and a larger proportion of their profits than ever before derive from keeping us that way. As a result, households in most Western countries have gone on a consumption binge: "I consume, therefore I am."

Savings rates in many Western countries have fallen to all-time lows. Greater social welfare, better macroeconomic management, and increased household wealth have certainly reduced the need to save for a rainy day. But increases in longevity, together with better health and lifestyle expectations, have at the same time increased the need to save for retirement. Numerous studies show that many people have undersaved, have underinvested, and are underinsured.

One of the problems is that the benefits of saving, investing, or buying insurance are, at best, deferred and intangible. They cannot be paraded at parties where we try to keep up with the Joneses.

The best example is the life insurance policy. Every year we receive a statement that shows our premiums and insured value, but we feel somehow cheated. We have paid for something we didn't use. We must literally die to realize the benefit of life insurance—and even then we will never see a return. No wonder insurance companies have a difficult time convincing people to buy their products!

Investing in life insurance requires us to look at the values behind it: our love for our families and our desire to leave them safe and secure.

THE DARK SIDE OF CONSPICUOUS CONSUMPTION

Psychologist Richard Ryan, in his foreword to Tim Kasser's *The High Price of Materialism*, notes that vast numbers of people have been seduced into believing that having more wealth and possessions is essential to "the good life." It is considered uncool to voice the old cliché "Money doesn't buy you happiness."

Imagine being at your local country club as a colleague describes how they have just watched the World Cup in their newly installed home theater. Thanks to an easy credit plan provided by the vendor, the first repayments aren't even due for twelve months!

Someone else is talking about his or her latest BMW. Your golf buddy has just spent a fortune on the best high-tech clubs that money can buy. (The background white noise to all of this is the media coverage about moguls like Donald Trump and their latest billion-dollar deals.)

How would you feel saying to your friends that you spent your last bonus on topping up your savings, acquiring an investment plan, or buying disability insurance? This sort of behavior—if you felt brave enough to even say such a thing—is likely to leave you feeling left out just like Eileen did, as we learned in chapter 2.

If you say anything at all about your investments at social gatherings, chances are you will relay the story about the mining stock that rose 300 percent, or the surefire winners you are backing this year. Discussion about your long-term investment approach, steadily building your portfolio, and riding through cycles in markets (the easiest and most reliable way to increase your wealth) could even attract mild contempt.

REFLECTIONS: Do you have the self-confidence
to resist the crowd and do what is best for you?

Do You Have the "Right" Stuff?

Today, people are often judged not by whether they are worthwhile human
beings but whether they have the right clothes, the right car, and all the
other "right" stuff.

The yardstick is not simply having enough, but having more, measured
against those around us in real life and the pseudo-realities of the big
screen and other media. It's easy to lose perspective and forget that many
of the "happy" celebrities on the big screen are anything but happy.

Many goods today are thought of as positional, which means they
can be enjoyed only if others don't have them. They are used to confirm
the owner's position in society. Typically, fashion trends emerge in the
upper middle class and eventually filter their way through society, by
which time the upper class has moved on to the next big thing. Under
these rules of the game, it is not enough to dine at a nice restaurant or to
drive a nice car; it has to be the *best* restaurant or the *best* car. And what
is considered the *best* is constantly and·deliberately changing so that the
average person cannot keep up. These games are simply distractions from
what is important.

Advertisers play a huge role in defining what the "right" stuff is. The
gorgeous blonde in the miniskirt, draped over the hood of a sports car, is
there for one reason only: to convince potential male buyers that owning
the car will not only get them from A to B but will also attract beautiful
women. Sadly, sometimes it will.

Today's BMW will always be superseded by tomorrow's. But if, as for
many people, it's a pipe dream anyway, exposure to such pressure may leave
a sense of personal disappointment, even failure.

Similar techniques are used in the sale of financial products and services. While there's no sports car for the blonde to recline on, the hot funds

and stocks of the moment are linked with glamorous lifestyles, and the use of "top returns" in advertising these financial products is designed to make investors feel they are missing out.

Remember Sir Isaac Newton, and be warned. Consider also the example of Jim Clark, the founder of Netscape and other computer companies. Before he started Silicon Graphics, Clark said a fortune of $10 million would make him happy. Then he started Netscape, and was quoted as saying that $100 million would make him happy. By the time he founded Healtheon, the figure had been revised upward, to $1 billion. At that point, Clark started to compare his wealth with that of others, such as the founder of the Oracle software company. "Once I have more money than Larry Ellison, I'll be satisfied," he announced.

So how much is really enough? A strong focus on materialism does little to make us feel better. It not only fails to satisfy our psychological needs but also undermines important values. The really perverse thing is that material success can feel as disappointing as failure.

The Disease of Affluenza

If materialism contributes to unhappiness, unhappiness can also contribute to materialism. Psychology professor Kasser identifies an infectious illness he calls "affluenza," in which sufferers become addicted simply to having or consuming. This is closely connected with feelings of personal insecurity.

Today's four best-selling drugs are used to treat health problems that are mainly stress related: hypertension treatments, tranquilizers, sleeping pills, and antidepressants. Use of these drugs crosses all social and economic boundaries.

The petty, envious world of Eileen and Sinead and other modern-day adolescents is not so far from contemporary adult life after all. Defining and understanding our personal values is one of the keys to a practical rather than a slavish approach to possessions, and living our values is one of the sources of authentic happiness.

THE ANCESTRAL MIND
AND THE THINKING MIND

Much of the development of the human brain occurred with the emergence of hunter-gatherers on the African savannah 200,000 years ago. Our environment has changed in recent times so rapidly that it's been hard for our brains to keep up.

For example, when processing images from the eye, the brain assumes a simple relationship between the distance of an object and its clarity. If we see a lion clearly, the brain tells us that it's close, pumps up our adrenalin, and prepares us for fight or flight. On the other hand, if the image of the lion is blurred, the brain tells us it's too far away to worry about and to save precious energy while remaining sensibly alert.

Today, this phenomenon can lead to large multicar accidents on the freeway. During foggy conditions on any major interstate, motorists can mistakenly believe that because the car in front appears indistinct, it must be at a safe distance. They maintain their speed rather than slowing down. By the time that they realize their mistake, it may be too late. Of course, such accidents are easy to avoid. A driver simply needs to understand the illusion, override the automatic response, and not travel so close.

Likewise, the way our minds work doesn't exactly make it easy to stay focused on what's important. When our ancestors lived in caves, hunting and gathering by day and sleeping by night, life was short and brutal, but fairly simple. The first humans were confronted by limited choices: where to live, what to eat, whom to partner with. Instinct was the key to survival.

So abundant is material wealth in Western societies today, however, that for the first time, many people can easily satisfy these basic needs. Finding a balance between instinctive and thoughtful rational responses has become a new priority.

In his book *The Ancestral Mind*, Gregg Jacobs separates the human mind into two categories: the Ancestral Mind and the Thinking Mind peculiar to *Homo sapiens*.

The Ancestral Mind is from our preverbal past and is similar in function to the mind of a lizard. Charged with looking after fundamental well-being, it knows only base responses like fear and pain. The Ancestral Mind governs basic emotions that, psychologically, are a "preparation to act." Emotions are there for a reason: they move us to make decisions.

The Thinking Mind is the rational, conscious mind that processes information into complex, abstract thoughts. Such thoughts occur in the prefrontal cortex, which is involved in such advanced cognitive activities as reasoning, anticipation, and planning, as well as in organizing actions toward a goal.

The Ancestral Mind is, in a sense, what's left when the Thinking Mind is switched off. When you take an instant dislike to someone for no apparent reason, it's your Ancestral Mind at work. When, based on their actions, you decide you don't like people, your Thinking Mind is at work.

The Ancestral Mind is responsible for many of the instinctive but destructive investment behaviors that will be discussed in part 2. The psychological issues discussed here are often in the realm of the Thinking Mind.

Jacobs argues that "evolution has placed a higher priority on immediate emotional responses than on thinking, reflecting, and planning . . . If we always had to wait for the Thinking Mind to determine whether something is dangerous, we might not only be wrong—we might be dead."

In this regard, the Thinking Mind provides a counterbalance to instinct. However, it has a drawback. The Thinking Mind is prone to endless "mental chatter" and tends to give negative thoughts higher status, which can be destructive and distracting. Most importantly, it is the Thinking Mind that is behind responses such as envy and jealousy, which as we saw in the previous chapter play such a large part in the culture of consumerism. We might be living happily on an income of $60,000 per annum until we learn that our sister or neighbor earns an income of $120,000—with less responsibility.

For those who are motivated by material as opposed to nonmaterial goals, the troubling internal dialogue set off by such a discovery is likely to be louder and more persistent. This helps explain why the wealthiest people are often the least satisfied.

The Thinking Mind helps to counterbalance decision making that is based purely on instinct. Finding a balance between our Ancestral Mind and our Thinking Mind is another key to staying focused on what's important and, therefore, an enduring source of personal happiness.

CHOICE: ENOUGH IS ENOUGH?

Imagine what life would be like without an array of restaurants just around the corner from your office; new books or movies or music; vacations to anywhere; your favorite dessert; or simply a cup of coffee made just the way you like it.

There is an extraordinary range of choices in modern life compared with lifestyles as recent as a hundred—or even fifty—years ago. Choice, and our ability to exercise it, is an important part of our freedom; it enhances our sense of being in control of our destiny.

It is possible, however, to have too much of a good thing. When we navigate the endless rows of supermarket shelves and contend with dozens of types of breakfast cereals, shampoos, baby foods, "healthy" olive oils, pasta sauces, and boxes of prepared meals, excessive choice may well cause paralysis rather than joy. Without an advanced degree in actuarial science, anyone who has had to choose between different cell phone plans will know the feeling of confusion and "missing out" that may result.

On average, Americans now encounter three thousand advertisements every day that tell them what they can acquire. Given such a glut of options, how can we hope to choose wisely?

Psychologist Barry Schwartz has explored the paradox that too much choice might be a bad thing. He identifies two key consumer types: *maximizers* and *satisficers*.

Choice is especially hard for maximizers, who always seek out the best. They spend hours, days, even weeks wading through all the possible choices. When they make a selection, they often descend into feelings of regret when something "better" becomes available.

Maximizers have a particularly hard time with products such as computers. They feel compelled to test everything available and take longer to make decisions—if they make any kind of decision at all. Although objectively they may end up with better results, they are usually less satisfied in the long run. "They are also less happy with life in general, less optimistic and more depressed," Dr. Schwartz tells us.

Drawing on research undertaken by Columbia Business School professor Sheena Iyengar, Schwartz found that shoppers were ten times as likely to buy jam when only six varieties were on display as when there were twenty four. Similarly, when the number of ways in which people could save for retirement went up, the likelihood that they would choose to save at all went down.

In the world of investment markets, this is a serious issue. For would-be maximizers, given that there are thousands of readily available investment options and that it is impossible to forecast which one(s) will perform best, grief is almost guaranteed.

Satisficers, by contrast, settle for "good enough." They stop searching once they have found something that serves their purpose. They suffer less long-term regret than maximizers do, and they waste less time and go home happy.

How will you deal with the extraordinary range of available choices, which can be either a source of disappointment or a contributor to happiness? You will be happier as a satisficer rather than a maximizer. Satisficers understand what is important; they understand the idea of HOC and do not waste time on irrelevant trifles and distractions. They are therefore more likely to capture the Happiness Prize.

REFLECTIONS: Are you more like a maximizer or a satisficer? What about your partner? Does your personal style help you to deal with the multitude of choices available in today's world, or is it a hindrance?

STRATEGIES FOR AUTHENTIC HAPPINESS

The positive psychology movement that has emerged in the past fifteen years emphasizes the importance of individuals taking control of their psychological health.

The leaders of this movement include Martin Seligman and Tal Ben-Shahar, professors of psychology at the University of Pennsylvania and Harvard, respectively. Increasingly, their work is overlapping with those whose exploration of happiness has been from a spiritual perspective, such as French research-scientist-turned-monk Matthieu Ricard.

They build on the work of the late Abraham Maslow, the father of humanistic psychology, for whom self-actualization represented the pinnacle of psychological health. People who achieve this state are motivated by a desire for personal growth, meaning, and beauty, rather than by insecurity and attempts to fit in with the expectations of others. (Here again we could cite the example of Warren Buffett. One of the keys to his success in life and as an investor in the stock market is that he has not conformed to the expectations of others. He has chosen his own authentic path—despite being criticized for doing so.)

These modern pioneers draw on far more theoretical and empirical research than was available to Maslow, and as a result they provide a more comprehensive understanding of what happiness really is. Dr. Seligman's main idea is that there are several routes to authentic happiness, each very different. He distinguishes between *pleasures* and *gratifications*. Pleasures are momentary and are further divided into bodily and higher pleasures. *Bodily pleasures* come from external stimuli that bring immediate delight to the senses. They may come from eating chocolate, having a warm bath on a cold day, hearing a few bars from your favorite song. *Higher, more complex pleasures* include feelings like euphoria, hilarity, or ecstasy. A great comedy routine or an unforgettable concert may be sources of higher pleasure.

Gratifications draw on our personal strengths. They involve engaging in an activity that is challenging and requires skill and concentration. There are clear goals, with immediate feedback on how we are doing. Our involvement in the activity is deep, can seem effortless, and gives us a sense of control. Gratifications are limitless: horseback riding, playing chess, writing, dancing, mustering cattle, painting, or teaching, to name but a few. Rather than merely stimulating our emotions, the deep sense of involvement we have while doing these activities evokes a feeling of flow, in which our sense of self disappears, time stops, and we live for the moment.

Gratifications come about through the exercise of our strengths and virtues. Understanding the distinction between momentary pleasures and rewarding gratifications is one of the greatest opportunities for hedonic arbitrage, which we introduced earlier in this chapter. In a nutshell, the idea is that we are best off spending our limited money on those things that make the biggest contribution to our happiness. Not only do the gratifications have a longer-lasting impact on happiness, because they come about through the exercise of our strengths and virtues, they also typically cost us less.

By organizing your life to have an abundance of both pleasures and gratifications, you can attain happiness. Be aware, however, that we become used to the momentary pleasures quickly. The second sip of a great wine or the second week of driving a new sports car brings far less pleasure than the first sip or week did. To some extent pleasures can be enhanced by techniques such as spacing and savoring. For example, this may involve taking time between sips of that exceptional wine, making yourself conscious of the taste of the drink in your mouth, and sharing the same experience with others. But there are limits.

Our neurons are wired to respond to novel events, not to those that provide no new information. The danger for people who do not realize this is that they devote their lives to loveless sex, binge-drinking, shopping sprees, or drug taking in the belief that greater frequency will compensate for the diminished thrill of each individual activity. This drains the time and energy we have to discover gratifications, the lasting sources of happiness. Also central to the good life is the idea of positive emotion. Research by Barbara Fredrickson shows that positive emotion has played an important role in evolution. When we are in a positive mood, we find it easier to forge friendships, find love, and form alliances. Mentally we are more expansive, tolerant, and creative, making us more open to new ideas and experience, compared with the constrictions of negative emotion.

Positive emotion works in the past, present, and future. Contentment is a positive emotion relating to our pasts. It can be increased through gratitude, forgiveness, and freeing ourselves from stifling ideologies that presuppose the world works in only one way or that there is only one path to salvation.

By learning to recognize and dispute the pessimistic thoughts against which we all struggle, positive emotion about the future, such as optimism, can be increased. Much of today's cognitive behavioral therapy, offered as a mainstream treatment for conditions such as depression and anxiety, is focused on this very insight. But you do not need to be unwell to increase your optimism.

Most of us don't need much help finding what brings us immediate pleasure. Figuring out what will give us a sense of gratification, on the other hand, requires that we identify our signature strengths. Seligman identifies twenty four "ubiquitous strengths," including our ability to love, forgive, appreciate beauty, be kind, be optimistic, and be curious. Our signature strengths are the ones we are best at. When using these strengths, we have a real sense of ownership and authenticity ("it's the real me") and a sense of excitement and invigoration rather than exhaustion. (To find out more about signature strengths, visit our website, www.howmuchisenough.net.)

In *Finding Flow*, 2000 Thinker of the Year recipient Mihaly Csikszentmihalyi first explored the concept of flow that Seligman associates with gratifications. This is similar to what Maslow described as the "peak experience" that he often found in emotionally healthy individuals who were "self-actualized," that is, who reported feeling moments of great awe or bliss.

Flow experiences, which involve transcending our sense of self, are closely linked to that idea of self-actualization. True flow experiences typically occur when we are doing something for the sheer enjoyment of it. We become less aware of ourselves because we are so immersed in the activity. Children are usually better at this than adults are, and their play is one of the best examples of such experiences.

Flow experiences can occur during any number of the activities Seligman listed as gratifications. One reason for the emerging popularity in Western societies of disciplines such as yoga is the search for flow experiences removed from day-to-day life.

Highly engaged conversations and stimulating work produce similar effects. One of the greatest bonuses in life is if you can build flow into your work. For this to occur you need to approach what you do as a calling, with passionate commitment to the work for its own sake. The good news is that people in even the most basic jobs can feel this sense.

For example, Seligman recalls that when he visited a close friend who lay in a coma on life support, a hospital orderly was hanging pictures on the wall of his friend's room. When asked what he was doing, the man replied, "I'm an orderly on this floor, but I bring in new prints and photos every week. You see, I'm responsible for the health of all these patients.

Take Mr. Miller here. He hasn't woken up since they brought him in, but when he does, I want to make sure he sees beautiful things straight away."

As Seligman observes, the orderly "did not define his work as the emptying of bedpans or the swabbing of trays, but as protecting the health of his patients and procuring objects to fill this difficult time of their lives with beauty. He may have held a lowly job, but he re-crafted it into a high calling."

REFLECTIONS: Spend five minutes thinking about how you can re-craft your work in a similar way. It doesn't matter whether you are in paid employment, bringing up children, or retired and doing volunteer work. The same principles apply.

Do you really believe in what you are doing and feel you are achieving something? If your work causes harm to people, such as a job in the tobacco industry, and other options are freely available, then the re-crafting we suggest may be impossible. In that case, one of the most positive things you can do to improve your well-being is to change jobs.

We need to pursue activities for their own sake, not for reward or praise. It's the journey that matters, not the destination.

Capturing the Happiness Prize will involve combining many different pleasures, taken in moderation, with an abundance of gratifications. Our signature strengths are used as often as possible, in particular in the great arenas of life: work, love, and parenting. Beyond the good life, however, *is* the meaningful life, in which we use our signature strengths in the service of something larger than we are. In chapter 6 we provide some inspiring examples of people who are doing just that.

The Rat Racer, the Hedonist, and the Nihilist

Dr. Ben-Shahar emphasizes that happy people try to live life by pursuing activities that bring enjoyment now, but also lead to a fulfilling future. If you are a student who loves learning, for example, you may enjoy discovering new ideas while also building a productive long-term career. Those who work at something they love—whether it is medicine, business, or art—can enjoy the journey as well as the destination.

In contrast, there are three archetypes who fail to get this relationship right: the rat racers, the hedonists, and the nihilists.

Rat racers are those who, rather than enjoying the present, keep focused on the achievement of a future goal that they are convinced will make them happy. From a young age in our homes, at school, and certainly as adults at work, we are rewarded for results rather than journeys. We learn to focus on the next goal rather than on our present experience and can, like Roger and Heather in the previous chapter, chase the ever-elusive future our entire lives.

Being a hard worker or a high achiever is not synonymous with being a rat racer, however. Many hardworking people derive great joy from their work, whereas rat racers do not. They believe, instead, that once they reach a certain destination, they will be happy. The rat racer's challenge is to devote his or her energies to the right activities—those that create a sense of both current and future benefit.

In contrast, the hedonist is always on the lookout for instant gratification. There is an element of this in all of us. Yet a life based only on hedonism lacks the flow associated with gratifications and can therefore be a bit meaningless.

Dr. Csikszentmihalyi says the best moments in a person's life "usually occur when a person's body or mind is stretched to its limits in a voluntary effort to accomplish something difficult and worthwhile." The hedonist's challenge is to discover the more enduring sources of happiness.

Finally, the nihilist is someone who has given up on happiness or is resigned to the belief that life has no meaning. The nihilist needs to develop an understanding of the sources of happiness and how these may be applied.

In building a personal Bridge of Well-being, it's important to concentrate on enjoying the journey and not be overly focused on its completion. Our aim is to maximize our enjoyment of what we do today while seeing that it contributes to a worthwhile future purpose.

Happy people experience highs and lows like everyone else. However, their overall state of being is positive, and whatever trials and losses they encounter are ultimately outweighed by the joy of living.

The next chapter proposes some simple, practical ways you can put the insights about happiness drawn from this chapter to work in your daily life.

Chapter 4

STRATEGIES FOR WELL-BEING

THE TOTAL NUMBER OF MILLIONAIRES who emerged in history up to about 1900 is probably less than the total number of new millionaires who arise each year in the USA today. In this context, it's especially important to develop a *philosophy* of money, one that focuses on intrinsic, not material, needs.

Financial decisions are influenced heavily by our circumstances, emotions, and values, and grappling with these issues is something each of us must do ourselves. No set of "hot tips" will necessarily help.

The major religions of the world, to which people traditionally turn for guidance, aren't much help at charting a path. While they have plenty to say on beliefs, philosophy, and values, they tend to take a black-and-white view about money.

SEARCH FOR WELL-BEING

Theologian and reformer Martin Luther left no doubt about his view of the role of money when he wrote the following in 1566: "Wealth has in it neither material, formal, efficient, nor final cause, nor anything else that is good; therefore our Lord God commonly gives riches to those from whom he withholds spiritual good."

This judgmental attitude is displayed by many of today's religious leaders. But mere condemnation of wealth provides little practical guidance concerning how to manage it.

Drawing on the latest psychological research and our experience with individuals worldwide, we can highlight some elements of a philosophy that helps an individual consider the role of money in a life filled with meaning and purpose. A life, in other words, that allows us to capture the Ultimate Prize.

In trying to apply the ideas in this chapter, be aware that change, especially of deeply ingrained habits, takes time. Ben-Shahar suggests that one of the best ways to overcome this is to ritualize the right activities. For example, because we value hygiene, we ingrain in our children the habit of brushing their teeth twice a day, washing their hands before they eat, and so on. Practicing these rituals makes the right behaviors automatic.

Similarly, we can turn activities that we want to engage in into habits, and we can introduce "negative rituals" into our lives: that is, times during which we refrain from doing certain things, such as using our cell phone, surfing the Internet, and so on.

Understand and Define Your Values

Successful people, almost without exception, have a well-developed sense of values. Warren Buffett's belief system, for example, appears to be rooted in moderation: a sense of balance, humility, and common sense. It seems to have much in common with the philosophy of American retailer Sam Walton, who, although a billionaire, still drove an old pickup truck, not as an affectation but because it was part of who he was and where he had come from.

Buffett's ability to follow his own path, and to avoid the traps of peer pressure and consumerism, is notable in all facets of his behavior, from avoiding investment trends to ignoring fashion. In *The Real Warren Buffett*, James O'Loughlin illustrates how consistently this theme appears throughout the legendary investor's life. He writes: "Herding is not a form of conduct in which Buffett seeks shelter. He doesn't feel the need. He doesn't key his behavior off the behavior of others. Standing alone holds no fear for him; it never has. This is why he has the resolve to step away when prices deteriorate, why he glories in the loneliness of being logical."

O'Loughlin goes on: "In high school he wore sneakers all year round, even when it was snowing—'Most of us were trying to be like everyone else,' said a friend at the time. 'I think he liked being different'—while in later years he bought suits, five at a time, all in the same 'style,' which was no style at all."

The most striking example of Buffett's refusal to bow to social pressures could be found, however, in his living arrangements. Here he flouts one of the most fundamental of Western social conventions: "He is married to one woman, lives with another," writes O'Loughlin, "*and conducts public relationships with both.*"

REFLECTIONS: Warren Buffett's philosophy and lifestyle may not suit everyone, but they seem to work for Buffett. What works for you?

LEARN WHAT EXPERIENCES YOU REALLY VALUE   Happy, fulfilled people come to understand the types of experiences they value, and why. They recognize in advance the difficulty of being sure of what will make them truly happy. So they use methods such as trial and error or "try before you buy." A simple example would be to take the eating-out test. If you were given the choice among dining out at an expensive restaurant, having a cheap-and-cheerful night out with a group of colleagues, or cooking at home with some of your closest friends, which would you choose—and why?

Of course, there is no right answer to this question. Your answer will vary depending on such factors as when you are asked, and by whom. However, your response may well have as much to do with the ambience and people involved in each experience as the actual dollars spent.

Why not try each one of the dining experiences in the next few weeks, and take note of which you enjoy the most? Then try to explain why.

DIP YOUR TOE IN THE WATER BEFORE SWIMMING   Imagine you've just walked in from the beach, having enjoyed one of the best vacation days of your life and feeling particularly close to your family. The real estate catalog on the end table promises that all this can be acquired. You sign up for an apartment that happens to be for sale in that very resort complex.

Maybe this story has a happy ending and these perfect sunny days last forever. But equally likely is that over the coming years, the maintenance costs of the apartment become a burden, your tastes change, your family doesn't want to spend time there every summer—and suddenly you feel committed to vacations that aren't what they used to be. That glorious feeling you once had proves hard to recapture. In terms of maximizing well-being for you and your family, could that money be better spent?

You may be a person who loves the feel of driving a fast car: the roar of the engine, the way it hugs the corners at high speed. You've always wanted a Porsche and, despite the protests of your spouse, you buy one—even at the cost of other experiences for you and your family, since you're not seriously wealthy. After the initial euphoria, however, you discover that you can't actually drive at maximum speed in residential areas (where you live) or in rush hour traffic (when you commute every day).

By thinking through the issue more clearly, there is a great opportunity for hedonic arbitrage, or maximizing well-being for the money spent, as we discussed in chapter 3. Instead of rushing into expensive financial adventures like vacation apartments and fast cars, ask yourself what you really want out of the experience. Instead of buying the vacation apartment, for instance, you could take out a long-term lease. Instead of stretching to buy the Porsche, you could join a motor club that enables drivers to enjoy, quite cheaply and safely, the thrill of racing.

To bring this concept to life we recommend that you keep a diary and note at the end of each day what it was that made you particularly happy, and what had little effect. In particular, jot down a list of the things on which you spent money, and note which ones contributed to your happiness and which ones faded quickly from memory. You may choose to track this over a weekend. Just a few days of this process will have a big impact on how you spend both your time and your money.

Honestly rating different experiences and testing the water before plunging right in are simple, practical ways to gain a better understanding of what you truly value—and what you should, and can, afford to pay.

Focus on Intrinsic, Not Material Needs

Building on Maslow's hierarchy of needs, Dr. Kasser has identified four sets of needs that he proposes must be satisfied if human beings are to function well. They are needs for

- Safety, security, and sustenance
- Competence, efficacy, and self-esteem
- Connectedness
- Autonomy and authenticity

Well-being and quality of life increase when these four sets of needs are satisfied and decrease when they aren't.

Safety, security, and sustenance refer to needs we have for food, shelter, clothing, and a sense of protectedness—the essentials of life. These needs are mostly material, and without them life can be miserable. For the majority of people in Western societies, these needs are reasonably well met.

Competence, efficacy, and self-esteem involve feeling that we are capable of doing what we have set out to do, and that we can obtain the things we value.

Connectedness involves relating to others, the well-documented human need for closeness and intimacy. There's a reason why the words "sad" and "lonely" so often appear together.

Autonomy and authenticity involve being engaged in our lives, rather than merely going through the motions. We should strive for freedom and opportunities to experience life in our own way.

THE POWER OF LOVE AND FRIENDSHIP

Psychologists are unanimous about the importance of feeling connected. Sociologist Eckersley encapsulates this perfectly: "Well-being comes ... from being suspended in a web of relationships and interests which give meaning to our lives. The intimacy, belonging and support provided by close personal relationships seem to matter most; isolation exacts the highest price."

What is the best way to develop satisfying relationships? Here are some practical ways to get started.

Look after yourself. This does not mean being selfish or pampering yourself unnecessarily. But unless you cultivate self-respect and feel you are worthy of being loved, it is hard to be sincere in your feelings for anyone else.

In *Staying Sane in a Changing World*, Fortune 500 consultant Cairnes has identified sources of disabling beliefs that undercut self-esteem. You may not even be aware of these beliefs, but they are so ingrained that they deeply influence your behavior and self-confidence. They then prevent you from trying to form deep relationships, even though others might well find you attractive and worthwhile.

Do things you enjoy. Join organizations promoting activities that interest you. These could be sporting clubs, political parties, cooking classes, or community service organizations, to name but a few. "Engaging in activities, even alone, is often an essential first step in defeating loneliness," advises psychologist Antony Kidman in *From Thought to Action*.

Do things others enjoy. Interacting with others not only opens you up to new experiences but also helps you forge closer relationships with different people. In *The Happiness Handbook*, Sharp suggests that such engagement may lead to a virtuous cycle. When you do something nice for your partner, friends, or colleagues, improving their well-being, you also build your own feelings of satisfaction. This may range from buying flowers for your spouse or a bottle of wine for a friend, to simply turning off the TV and having a real conversation with your parents or children.

Be generous. Practice acts of kindness, such as visiting someone who is sick or elderly, phoning a person who is lonely, or making a "gratitude visit." In *Authentic Happiness,* Martin Seligman suggests that you could write a note of appreciation thanking someone important in your life to whom you owe a debt of gratitude. Then you could visit that person to read it to him or her. Sound corny? Perhaps. Hard to do? Probably. Rewarding? Almost certainly—for them, as well as for you.

In one of Seligman's classes, his students explored whether happiness comes more readily from the exercise of kindness than from having fun. The conclusion was that the afterglow of pleasurable activity paled in comparison with the effects of kind actions. Done in a genuine way, acts of kindness result in total engagement and a loss of self-consciousness, producing flow.

Share your feelings. Forging close relationships ultimately requires you to have the courage to disclose secrets about yourself, your feelings, and your vulnerabilities. If you are more open to others, they will often reciprocate.

In his book *Passionate Marriage,* sex therapist David Schnarch argues that to allow love and passion to grow in a relationship requires a shift in focus from the desire to be validated—seeking approval and praise—to the desire to be known. Both partners must be willing to disclose their innermost selves—even aspects that do not show them in the most favorable light. This process is essentially a continuous one, and a sex life that keeps getting better may be just one of many benefits, he says. By giving more, both partners also gain more.

Dr. Schnarch's research contradicts the contemporary notion that sex with just one long-term partner inevitably gets a bit stale and boring. On the contrary, if the relationship grows in a truly reciprocal way, then a casual affair with even the most exotic and sexy stranger is unlikely to produce anything close to a similar level of satisfaction.

TAKE TIME TO SAVOR LIFE

How we use our time may be the determinant of well-being that is easiest to improve according to Daniel Kahneman, who was awarded the Nobel Prize in Economic Sciences in 2002 for his work in the area of behavioral finance.

Similarly, Kasser's research shows that time affluence is a consistent predictor of well-being, whereas material affluence is not. Time affluence means feeling that there is time to pursue activities that are personally meaningful, to reflect, to relax, and to educate oneself. Time poverty is the feeling that one is constantly stressed, rushed, overworked, and juggling too many competing priorities. Most of us feel this to some degree.

REFLECTIONS: Think of all the things that you
enjoy doing that you were able to do during the last week.
Has the sense of being pressed for time lessened your
sense of enjoyment? Do you find that the more you try
to pack into a day, the less you enjoy everything?

There is no way around this other than simplifying our lives and understanding that sometimes less is more. We need to plan and prioritize, and our priorities should be based on the pillars that make up our Bridge of Well-Being: namely, the values and goals we have defined, the resources we have applied to achieve our goals, and the investment strategy we have developed. In particular, our priorities should reflect what we value most. As Barry Schwartz says to both maximizers and satisficers alike, "Expect less. Settle for what is good enough. And then relax."

Become a Better Time Manager

Look at your desk calendar for next week. More than likely, it is full of activities, so it will be easy to decline all but the most urgent appointments. Two months out, however, your calendar is likely to be quite empty. This is why a favorite trick among salespeople is to ask for an appointment weeks or months in advance, knowing you are much more likely to accept. As the time for the appointment approaches, of course, you are as busy as always and curse yourself for having scheduled the appointment.

Part of our evolutionary legacy is that we place too little value on time in the future and end up wondering where our lives went. One way to deal with this is to fill your calendar only with important, as opposed to urgent, activities a year in advance.

This provides the opportunity to make a habit of things that are important in our lives. It could be a weekly tennis game, vacations with the family or friends, monthly catch-ups with your inner circle of acquaintances, quiet times for yourself, or whatever is important to you.

Another useful habit is to develop a "third place" where you can make the transition from a busy workplace to the less frantic pace of home. This may well be the drive or ride home from work. Learn to switch off your cell phone during this transition and at home. Even if you have to switch it on later in the evening, this simple practice will help ensure that you are truly "present" with the people you love.

Remember, the wine connoisseur does not gulp an entire glass of wine. To become a life connoisseur, we too need to take our time.

Learn to Relax and Look Within

The relaxation response, documented in any good stress-management book, is the most direct route to clearing away endless mental chatter and improving your ability to concentrate. No one can live continuously on adrenalin without paying a price. Over time, a heightened sense of calm from relaxation will extend throughout the day, serving as a foundation for a more positive outlook on life. The relaxation response, based on simple breathing techniques, is one safe and tested way to open our valves and release their pressure.

Part of improving your ability to relax involves preparing well for the inevitable periods of stress you will encounter. Laying the foundations before the next stressful period strikes will make it easier to maintain your health. This is because it is not the existence of pressure, but your response to it, that determines whether stress turns to distress or is channeled into positive energy. Stress itself is not bad—it's how you manage stress that matters.

The Happiness Institute has identified a number of simple, practical strategies to help you ward off the negative effects of stress, cultivate an ability to relax, and promote living in the moment. The technique of mindfulness is based on Buddhist approaches to meditation, and rather than simply relating to relaxation, it relates to living wholly and consciously within the moment. Most of our lives are spent thinking about the past and the future, which means we are at risk of missing out on an intensity of experience in the here and now.

Here are some examples of mindfulness exercises.

- **One-minute exercise.** Sit in front of a clock or a watch that you can use to time the passing of one minute. Your task is to focus your entire attention on your breathing, and nothing else, for every second of the minute.

- **Mindful eating.** This involves sitting down at a table and eating a meal without engaging in any other activities—do not read a newspaper or book, watch TV, listen to the radio, or talk. Pay attention to each piece of food: how it looks, how it smells, how you cut the food, the muscles you use to raise your fork to your mouth, and the texture and taste of the food as you chew it, slowly. You will be amazed at how different food tastes when eaten in this way and how filling (and enjoyable) a meal can be.

- **Mindful walking.** This is a variation on mindful eating. As you walk, concentrate on the feel of the ground under your feet, as well as your breathing. Observe the scene around you, staying in the moment. Let your other thoughts go: look at the sky, the view, the foliage; feel the wind, the temperature of your skin; enjoy the moment.

The focus on the inner self is important because, as Matthieu Ricard has found, happiness is not about things or activities. It is a state of profound emotional balance. A person who achieves this state can withstand periods of physical and mental suffering without losing his or her sense of fulfilment.

"A storm may be raging at the surface, but the depths remain calm," Dr. Ricard says. "The wise man always remains connected to the depths.

On the other hand, he who knows only the surface and is unaware of the depths is lost when he is buffeted by the waves of suffering."

Reframe in Happiness Terms

Understanding how much is enough to live a good life is essential to capturing the Happiness Prize. It is closely related to the fulfilment of personal values.

Looking once again at the concept of hedonic arbitrage may help us to do this. Professor Benartzi gives the example of a buyer comparing two similar models of BMW. The deluxe version costs $15,000 more than the basic model, but it has slightly superior features. When simply comparing the two models, people naturally prefer those superior features. But when the comparison is framed differently—for example, recognizing that the $15,000 can buy three years' worth of gasoline or enough to pay for several years of vacations and weekends away—then the result may well be different. In fact, Benartzi's research shows that in the latter case, buyers are much more likely to consider the basic model sufficient for their needs. Most people simply do not consider what else that $15,000 could buy, which highlights how important the issue of how we frame decisions is for our happiness.

REFLECTIONS: If you are planning a major expenditure, such as a kitchen or bathroom renovation, have you considered how else you might spend all, or part of, the money? Which alternative would contribute most to your happiness?

Through studying the psychological literature, it is hard to escape the conclusion that long-term success with money, including investing, is impossible to separate from success in life. Financial security and independence are important to most successful people. But the real challenge is finding a healthy balance between this and other important values such as authenticity, competence, and belonging.

Successful people use the power of the Thinking Mind for the rational analysis that is so important to making sound financial decisions. But they will also be able to call on the calming influence of the Ancestral Mind to switch off the endless noise of the Thinking Mind, with its capacity to create doubt and anxiety. A philosophy based on a healthy mix of values, the ability to use both the Thinking Mind and the Ancestral Mind, and being a satisficer rather than a maximizer are all factors that contribute to enduring happiness and fulfilment.

In the next chapter we look at the role of money in our lives and work, and what values we would like to pass on to our children. The values and goals you hold, and pass on, will provide the next generation with the emotional resilience to resist the siren call of the media, the Joneses, and the distractions caused by fear, greed, and envy.

Chapter 5

KIDS, MONEY, AND HAPPINESS

As we learned in chapter 2, the attitudes we absorb about money and happiness are shaped from our earliest childhood, most often modeled on the behavior of our parents and the other adults who influenced us. As parents, grandparents, aunts, uncles, teachers, and friends, we need to consider our answers to the questions raised in *How Much Is Enough?* in order to help us help the next generation.

BRINGING UP RESILIENT, SUCCESSFUL KIDS

Most of us can relate to stories about children who have been "given everything" yet have ended up with little direction in life. One of the paradoxes of affluence is that it produces kids who are remarkably sophisticated and spoiled, while at the same time are more dependent, anxious, and directionless. They are unaware of the deeper sources of happiness or the values and thinking necessary to experience the Ultimate Prize.

Bringing up kids who are emotionally resilient and financially successful—who have a strong sense of their own values and an intuitive understanding of the relationship between money and happiness—is a huge challenge for today's parents.

Most people would agree on at least one common goal for our children: we want them to enjoy a sense of well-being. By this we mean holistic well-being, from emotional and physical health to success in pursuing their passions and career paths, as well as having enough money.

Our education system focuses primarily on skills that lead to good academic results and material success. While important, these things are not directly linked to achieving a sense of well-being. Stephen Meek, the headmaster of Geelong Grammar School in Victoria, Australia, which has a long-standing reputation for leadership in education, is establishing a Well-Being Center at the school, with the support of academics from the University of Pennsylvania. A substantial investment has been made to develop courses for students and to train teachers in applying happiness concepts in teaching their own subjects.

This is a rare example. In most cases, parents are the main guides in teaching their children about well-being. Combining our own experience with the latest behavioral research leads us to question whether some common parenting practices are, in fact, the best way to help our kids.

Dealing with the Burden of Affluence

No one would ever choose to be born into poverty. However, being born into affluence is no guarantee that you will lead a fulfilling life. The need to work hard, to budget, and to consider what is important to you before spending money will help you develop values and skills.

In affluent households where parents may try to protect their children from hardships to which they themselves were exposed, there may be less opportunity to develop these life skills. As a result, these children may be robbed of the opportunity to feel a true sense of achievement.

Consider the universal saying "From shirtsleeves to shirtsleeves in three generations." It is important not to let affluence rob your children of the opportunity to achieve, nor to undervalue the valuable skills that are learned from perseverance and hard work.

For Love or Money?

A common goal for education in rich families is to set the kids on the path that leads to the highest-paying career, typically in areas like finance, law, or medicine. Children are encouraged to choose subjects that enable them to maximize their grades in university entrance exams and access the "best" courses. As a result, enrollments at business schools have boomed in the past twenty years while arts faculties at major universities have shrunk.

Once their children's careers have begun, the parents expect the young adults to marry and start a family and follow the well-worn path to happiness that they believe comes with material comfort. Just as an arranged marriage may lead to everlasting love, for many people this path of "arranged education" works out satisfactorily. For a lucky minority, it provides an opportunity to discover skills and passions they never knew they had.

For a less-fortunate majority, however, overt pressure to pursue a high-status career path can lead to disillusionment, dissatisfaction, and in some cases, disaster. We have all seen examples of this.

This pressure is manifested in stress and anxiety among adolescents, high dropout rates at universities, and radical midstream career switching. In some recorded cases, people in their forties and fifties who are outwardly successful have expressed feelings of having wasted their work lives pursuing someone else's dream.

An alternative approach to education involves providing girls and boys with opportunities to explore the relationship among three core areas that are important to lasting fulfilment. As shown in the figure at the top of the next page, these are

- What they are passionate about
- What they are good at
- How they can make sufficient money

PASSIONS, COMPETENCE, AND MONEY

The figure at the top of the next page shows that all three factors—passions, competence, and money—are important, and that financial security and happiness are likely to increase if we focus our goals on where the circles overlap.

The starting point, however, should be to help our children discover their passions. As Abraham Maslow wrote, "The most beautiful fate, the

The dynamic relationships between passions, competence, and money

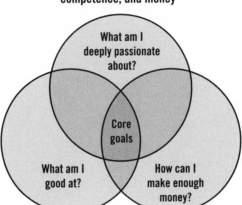

most wonderful good fortune that can happen to any human being, is to be paid for doing that which he passionately loves to do."

The role of parents is not to dictate but to create a nurturing environment that enables children to develop an understanding of these relationships for themselves. Here is what you might say during an all-important discussion with your son or daughter about choosing meaningful work.

> You asked me what you should think about when considering a career. There are three things I wish for you, in whatever you choose to do. First, you should truly enjoy your work so that it gives you a real sense of satisfaction. You will spend a large part of your life working, and the quality of your life will be greatly enhanced if you are doing something that you really enjoy.
>
> Second, I hope that in your career and in your life you will make a positive difference in the lives of other people and the community. The sense of doing something worthwhile for others, even for profit, greatly enhances your sense of satisfaction. It gives you the opportunity to lead a meaningful life, not just a good life.

Finally, I hope that you choose a career where you can earn enough money to provide you and your family with a comfortable living. With enough for your needs and happiness, you won't suffer debilitating fear and insecurity. But remember that security and well-being depend on how sensibly you spend, save, and invest your money, as much as on how much you earn and what you buy and own. And this means you need to think carefully about what will make you happy.

REFLECTIONS: What do you say to your children about money and meaningful work?

Cultivating a Love of Learning

We can start to help our children by cultivating a love of learning that isn't motivated by exams, grades, and prizes. All of these do play an important role in education, but for many kids, it is important for public affirmation to be balanced by a private, home environment that encourages independent inquiry. We want to help our children discover what moves and inspires them.

Mihaly Csikszentmihalyi, as quoted by Tal Ben-Sahar in *Happier*, said: "Neither parents nor schools are very effective at teaching the young to find pleasure in the right things . . . [We] make serious tasks seem dull and hard, and frivolous ones exciting and easy. Schools generally fail to teach how exciting, how mesmerizingly beautiful science or mathematics can be; they teach the routine of literature or history rather than the adventure."

We need to help make our children aware of the different sources of happiness, of the distinction between short-lasting pleasures and longer-lasting gratifications, as well as the power of giving. We have worked with schoolchildren, getting them to do simple exercises in which they rate the happiness they get out of various material pleasures compared to activities that produce a sense of gratification. As awareness of how to capture the Happiness Prize builds, the child will intuitively modify his or her own behavior and values.

As part of following this approach with your own children, you can

- **Share your passions.** Have you ever developed an interest or hobby purely as a result of the infectious nature of a friend's passion and interest? Or perhaps you have developed an interest in history, mathematics, or a language because you learned from a teacher whose subject area was more than just a job.

  It is wonderful to have passions and interests in common with your children. Sharing your passions, however, is not a means of forcing them to love what you love. But enthusiasm is infectious, and your passions should simply open doors for your children through which they may choose to step of their own accord. We have pursued different careers from our parents, but they shared with us their love of reading and learning, which has positively influenced our paths in life.

- **Buy your children experiences as gifts.** In a society where so many people, including many children, have every material possession they need, research suggests that both the giver and the recipient are likely to get more satisfaction from an experience than receiving another "thing." The enjoyment of experiences lasts a lot longer, and when that experience is shared, it tends to contribute to deeper personal relationships as well.

  This does not mean, of course, that kids should not get that new bicycle or computer. Other gifts, however, could include classes in art, writing, photography, horseback riding, dancing, cooking, science, or singing. Others may include concert tickets, a weekend adventure, a mystery flight, or even a special lunch or dinner.

- **Explore different experiences, cultures, and places.** Vacation resorts are great places to unwind, but not to experience the world. On the other hand, travel to foreign countries, especially developing countries, can be a powerful educational experience. Within the borders of your country, too, there might be ways to expose children to different people, such as visits to farms or fishing villages or Indian reservations. Adventures such as mountaineering, hiking, canoeing, cycling, or attending music and dance festivals can also provide children with new experiences.

- **Give your children the opportunity to explore the natural world.**
  Exploring nature helps many youngsters develop a spirit of inquis-
  itiveness. This is because the natural world is so extraordinary and
  complex. This works even better if you yourself have a passion for the
  outdoors. Communing with nature does not have to mean hiking
  or camping in Alaska or Hawaii. It can simply involve a trip to the
  beach, a walk in a regional park, or staying up late at night to watch
  the stars come out.

Letting Passions Guide Skills

While our genes predispose us to be good at certain things, practicing a
skill for just twenty to thirty minutes a day can also turn us into experts. So
don't be too quick to prejudge what your children are capable of learning
based on their "natural aptitude."

The most useful tools for developing new skills are desire and necessity.
For example, most people fear public speaking almost as much as death.
Neither of us considers himself a "natural" public speaker, yet during our
careers we have each been forced to develop this skill to a fair degree of
competence in order to share ideas and achieve success with others.

Marathon swimmer Susie Maroney suffered from asthma as a child and
took up swimming to reduce its debilitating effects. She developed such
a passion for the water that she broke endurance race records around the
world. Her achievements include numerous crossings of the English Chan-
nel, as well as winning the famous Manhattan Island swim three times.

Similarly, the greatest Olympic swimmer of all time, Michael Phelps,
found that his routine in the pool was the key to overcoming the attention
deficit disorder problems he suffered from as a child.

Internationally acclaimed Italian tenor Andrea Bocelli was born with
congenital glaucoma, and by the age of twelve he had become blind. This
has not stopped him from performing around the world for millions of
fans, and selling tens of millions of albums.

Passion will not always be enough, of course. In some cases there is
too great a gap between one's passion in a field and the talent needed to
achieve significant success. However, one of the beauties of the modern

world is the ability to combine different passions and skills in creative and fulfilling ways.

REFLECTIONS: Can you think of any skills that you have learned that, previously, you did not know you were capable of? What motivated you to develop those skills?

DEVELOPING FINANCIAL KNOW-HOW

It has been said, "Any man who is not a socialist at age twenty has no heart—but any man who is still a socialist at age forty has no brain." This captures the natural inclination of younger people to lean toward idealism, while older people tend toward the pragmatism gained from experience.

Young people who have the idealism to pursue lives as revolutionaries, artists, or poets—even if they live in poverty—have charisma, and they can sometimes make us feel old and cynical. As life moves on, however, being able to earn enough money becomes an important contributor to a person's well-being. We have all heard stories of young idealists who ended up bitter and poor.

Developing financial literacy and basic commercial skills is now recognized as an important part of every child's education. Our challenge is not to reduce every activity or achievement to money. A child's main motivation should be to pursue activities that generate a love of life.

How Money Has Become "Invisible"

One of the challenges involved in teaching money skills is that, in the words of financial literacy guru Paul Clitheroe, "money has become invisible." In traditional working-class societies, the weekly wage was placed in different jam jars, each labeled for a specific purpose: "Rent," "Food," "Clothes," and so on. It was easy for everyone in the family to see where the money came from and exactly where the family finances stood at any given time. Today it is easy for children to believe that money comes, without limit, from a machine in the wall, or from a cashier at the supermarket.

When we say that we can't afford to buy our child a particular toy, how often do we then hear them ask, "Can't you just use your credit card?" Part of teaching our children how to develop an appreciation of the value of money is explaining where it comes from and how it flows through the household. This means coming to terms with the "B" word: budgeting.

Teaching Children Budgeting Skills

One of the best ways to teach children these skills is to give them responsibility for some or all of their discretionary spending. This can begin as early as ten years of age, or perhaps even earlier. One approach is to create the Family Bank.

Each month (weekly if the child is younger, quarterly if older), you pay an allowance into this bank. The child is then responsible for paying for items such as casual clothes, movies, toys, and sweets.

You can produce a simple monthly statement for each child, showing their balances and how much they have withdrawn. To encourage savings discipline, you may offer a matching bonus for any amount that is unspent at the end of the month.

The Family Bank requires each family member to observe a few basic rules if it is to work properly.

- Agree up front what counts as discretionary expenditure, taking into account the nature of the child. Generally, parents should pay for things like meals, basic household requirements, and educational fees and school needs, as well as other items necessary for the child's growth. If your child is fashion conscious, including clothes in their discretionary budget works well. If not, you may be better off making clothes your responsibility and leaving discretionary spending for treats alone.

- Create a system to track what is spent. Every time your child withdraws money from the Family Bank, jot it down on a piece of paper, and update the balance each month.

- Parents must have a disciplined approach. Your boss is unlikely to give you a pay raise just because you have spent more than your paycheck, so teach your children this lesson at an early age.

Children learn from role models, so if managing the family budget is not your greatest strength, it may be time to help yourself. Start with a basic budgeting book or budget planner, and as your experience increases, you can work your way toward a full-blown financial plan.

REFLECTIONS: What are your children's money skills and what will they have learned from observing their parents?

Teaching Basic Investment Literacy

Together with teaching children how to manage their spending habits to provide a foundation for smart money behavior, it is worth introducing them early to some other financial concepts. The precise age will vary depending on the child, but some key areas for most kids include

- How to find a balance between spending and saving
- The power of compound interest
- How the stock market works

As a society, we are not very good at long-term planning, saving, or investing. Nevertheless, these are important skills to learn if our children are to make good financial decisions throughout their lives.

The early teens are the time to get started. This is when control over money is becoming more important to them, and kids are able to understand more sophisticated concepts. One way to interest your teenagers at a time in their lives when there are many competing priorities is to help them set up a simple savings plan. This will demonstrate the power of compound interest with real money. They may contribute a few dollars a week to a savings account, for instance, and once their balance grows, they will start to appreciate the value of those regular interest payments.

Albert Einstein once observed that compound interest is the greatest miracle on Earth. Here are some simple facts that help explain why, which may help interest your children in this idea.

- $100 saved per month at zero interest for ten years results in a balance of $12,000.

- Invest this money and get a return of 5 percent, and the balance leaps to $15,093.

- If the return increases by a mere 1 percent, the balance increases to $15,817.

- If the interest is paid monthly, rather than yearly, then the balance increases to $16,388.

- If the money is invested for twenty years, at 6 percent per annum, compounding monthly, the balance leaps to $46,204.

This simple sequence highlights the power of time (hence the value of starting early); of getting the highest return for the level of risk; and of the frequency of compounding (hence the need to examine the details about the way a particular investment account works).

HOW YOUR KIDS CAN BUY A CAR IN JUST SIX YEARS   A powerful way of getting your teenagers to engage with their investment accounts is to set a goal. For many kids, having enough to buy a car at the end of high school is something worth striving for. Here's how it could work with a teenager who is starting junior high school and aiming, after six years, to buy a secondhand car worth $12,000.

Let's say you kick-start this special account with $1,500. The rest is up to your son or daughter. Don't contribute too much, even if you can afford it, or invaluable learning experiences will be lost. If the account earns no interest, the teenager needs to save $8,500 over six years, or around $4 per day. However, if he or she can invest the money in a money market account that pays interest at 5 percent, compounded monthly, the amount to save falls to around $3 per day. Put another way, by giving up a can or two of soda per day, the teen is well on the way to owning his or her first car.

There are many ways, of course, to change this example to fit in with your own son or daughter's circumstances. By taking on part-time work, he or she can shorten the time between now and having the car, buy a better one, or catch up after the early years of high school when it is harder to find work and save money. For some children, saving for their own piano or for a "gap year" studying overseas may provide a greater incentive.

More generally, this exercise will teach teenagers basic and invaluable financial planning skills. They will learn, for example, how easily they can save for something that will make a real difference in their lives, simply by cutting out a small amount of spending that has no real effect on their happiness. If you have helped them appreciate the value of experiences rather than things, they will recognize that the true value of a car is the freedom it provides, not as a status symbol.

Special note: The teenage edition of *How Much Is Enough?* contains a variety of exercises and case studies that will help your children in their quest for money and happiness (see www.howmuchisenough.net).

CAREER, MARRIAGE, AND FAITH

The most valuable thing you can bequeath to your children is not money, status, or education. It is unconditional love. This does not mean that parents should let children do whatever they want. A sense of responsibility and clear boundaries are important to foster in a child. What it does mean is that within the boundaries of decent behavior, the greatest gift you can give your child—or any other human being—is to love them for who they are, not for what you want them to be.

Very young kids are more likely to take risks, explore their surroundings, and develop faster if they are secure in the unconditional love of their parents. Similarly, the confidence of adolescents to be themselves can be significantly influenced by their parents' approval—or otherwise.

There are three key areas in which parents' love can support the development of a self-confident person: choice of career, marriage partner, and faith.

Many parents have strong views on the career they would like for their child. However, we have already seen that forcing a career on your children, rather than providing guidance and advice, is akin to a gamble on their happiness. One of the best ways to help your child is to foster creative and adaptive skills that will be far more valuable in the workplace than specific skills based on old work patterns.

In terms of marriage partners and faith, as Western countries become increasingly multicultural, the chances diminish that our children will marry people of similar cultural and religious backgrounds. The chances of children adopting different religious practices increase. While many of us simply accept this, others are troubled by it and some find it impossible to accept.

In our own office and social networks, relationships among Irish Catholics, Turkish Muslims, Lebanese Christians, Indian Hindus, and European Jews (among others) flourish. This is a wonderful aspect of living in a multicultural society.

In a surprising number of cases, however, the parents of one or both partners are unaware of these relationships, even when the partners live together. The reactions of such parents may vary from threatening to disown the child to the silent treatment, or more subtle comments of disapproval. These responses generally undermine the child's well-being and impact the happiness of the entire family.

While we may want to influence our child's choices, the choice ultimately is theirs. If they make a mistake, the self-confidence gained from the security of their parents' love will help them bounce back. An absence of self-confidence, however, can cripple someone for life.

The Drummer's Business

A friend and client of ours, Brendan Burwood, loved music and enjoyed playing the drums in local bands as a teenager. But he also recognized his career prospects in this field were limited, so he earned a bachelor's degree in business, majoring in marketing, which was another passion of his. After a brief stint gaining useful experience in the corporate world, Brendan realized that he wanted to work for himself, so he started a business that combined his passions. (This allowed him to operate in the zone where the three circles in our figure intersect.)

Because he was close to the music scene, he could see that there was a strong interest in compilation albums that bring together hit singles from different artists. Record companies were not exploiting this. Brendan combined his knowledge of music with his flair for marketing to create an independent record label focusing on such albums. Hard work, inspired by the fact that he was immersed in the music that he loved, together with his strength in marketing, led to steady success. By the time he was in his midthirties, Brendan had built one of the largest independent record companies in Australia, and he had expanded internationally.

He recognizes the loving support of his parents as giving him the courage to pursue his interests and then being able to connect these with a successful business in a creative and fulfilling way.

Bill Gates, Steve Jobs, and Matthieu Ricard

Among the most spectacular examples of passion leading to financial success are internationally known creative entrepreneurs Bill Gates and Steve Jobs.

As a teenager, Gates, highly intelligent and curious, had the vision that every business and nearly every household in developed countries could have a computer. Computers were his passion, but very early on he also demonstrated commercial savvy. When the first personal computer emerged, Gates and his friend Paul Allen saw an opportunity to lead the development of software.

Gates dropped out of Harvard Law School and cofounded Microsoft. The initial reaction of his parents to this turn of events was one of natural concern that their son should commit himself to such an unproven concept. But they recognized his passion and supported him, without imagining that Microsoft would emerge as one of the world's most powerful companies and make Gates the world's richest person.

As we describe in chapter 6, in recent years Gates's passions have led him and his wife to address the major inequities he sees in wealth and health in the world. He has discovered greater meaning in giving away his fortune than in making it.

In his 2005 commencement speech at Stanford University, fellow Silicon Valley billionaire Steve Jobs highlighted three key elements in his success. He spoke of the importance of loving what you do; the importance of persistence; and using the inevitability of his death to focus on what was really important.

Unlike Gates, whose parents were comfortably well off, Jobs was adopted by a working-class couple who promised his unwed teenage mother that they would send him to university. After six months at the prestigious Reed College, he realized he had no idea what he wanted to do with his life, and that the fees were eating up his parents' precious savings. He decided to drop out, while remaining unofficially on campus for another eighteen months, visiting classes that sounded interesting.

Despite having to sleep on the floor in friends' rooms, returning Coke bottles for the five-cent deposit to buy food, and walking across town every Sunday night to get one good meal a week at the Hare Krishna temple, he was having the time of his life. He simply let himself stumble into things, following his curiosity and intuition, which later proved priceless.

One of the best examples of the serendipity that Jobs cites is the calligraphy class he attended. He learned about typefaces, spacing, and letter combinations. He found it fascinating, even though he could see no practical application for it in his life at the time. Ten years later, he was able to incorporate it into the first Macintosh, making it the first computer with beautiful typography and adding to its iconic appeal.

Luckily for Jobs, he found what he loved to do early. He and Steve Wozniak started Apple in his parents' garage when he was twenty, and in ten years Apple grew into a $2-billion company with more than four thousand employees. But shortly after he turned thirty, following a disagreement with the board about the company's direction, he was very publicly fired. Initially devastated and humiliated, he contemplated quitting the industry. It then dawned on him that he still enjoyed what he did, and so he persisted. Freed of responsibilities at Apple, he was able to enter one of the most creative periods of his life, developing Pixar, now the world's most successful film animation studio. He also developed NeXT, which was later sold to Apple when he made a triumphant return to rescue and take to new heights the company he had cofounded.

It is instructive how, according to his 2005 Stanford commencement speech, Jobs uses the image of death to remain focused. The prospect of death is the most useful tool that helps him focus on what is truly important in life. As he puts it:

Your time is limited, so don't waste it living someone else's life. Don't be trapped by dogma—which is living with the results of other people's thinking. Don't let the noise of others' opinions drown out your own inner voice. . . . Have the courage to follow your heart and intuition. They somehow already know what you truly want to become.

Bill Gates and Steve Jobs followed their passions through unconventional career paths and ultimately achieved great personal wealth. Many people across the spectrum of society follow similar paths without becoming billionaires, or even wealthy, but they nevertheless enjoy equally fulfilling lives.

Matthieu Ricard transformed his passion into another kind of life altogether. By the age of twenty he had earned a doctorate in biology from the Pasteur Institute. His life in Paris was rich in variety and held great prospects for earning good money while engaged in valuable work. But something was not quite right. As Ricard said in his book *Happiness: A Guide to Developing Life's Most Important Skill*, "I had an idea of what I did not want—a meaningless life—but could not figure out what I wanted." The turning point was watching a documentary on Tibetan Buddhist masters. He saw that from all of them there emanated "a strikingly similar inner beauty, compassionate strength, and wisdom," despite their everyday lives as refugees. Ricard abandoned his career and the material world and joined a Buddhist monastery in Nepal, where he has been based ever since. He has come to know that happiness is not about things or activities. It is a state of profound emotional balance. A person who achieves this state can withstand periods of physical and mental suffering without losing their sense of fulfilment.

Ricard has applied his training in science to his search for spiritual enlightenment, using it to gain deeper insights into the nature and sources of happiness. He has collaborated with neuroscientist Richard Davidson at the University of Wisconsin–Madison on a series of brain tests with advanced meditators. As part of these experiments, Ricard was placed inside a noisy, claustrophobic MRI machine. Being inside this machine is for most people, even for a few minutes, a major ordeal that sometimes causes them to panic. Ricard spent more than three hours there, going through several kinds of meditation. The scientists were astonished to see him emerge relaxed and smiling, in a calm state confirmed by the brainwaves that the machine measured. Daniel Goleman, author of *Emotional Intelligence,* commented that this "bespeaks a special state of mind, a capacity for confronting life's ups and downs with equanimity, even joy." It even led the researchers to dub Ricard "the happiest man alive."

An Unconventional Mother Who Raised Extraordinary Children

By age thirty, Ann Dunham Sutoro was a single mother of two children living in Indonesia, far from her birthplace in Kansas. Arun met Ann in 1981, when she was thirty-eight, while he was doing research in Indonesia; she generously offered him a place to stay in her home in Jakarta. Well before this book was conceived, Ann challenged the conventional script for raising successful children.

One of Ann's children, a boy, came from a brief marriage to an African man when she was only eighteen, and her daughter came from a similarly short-lived marriage to an Indonesian. I never met Ann's son, who was studying in America, but I sometimes read books to her ten-year-old daughter. Conventional wisdom would suggest that prospects for the children were limited. But Ann was ahead of her time and had a script of her own.

She bestowed great love on her children, but also had high expectations of them. She did not expect a particular career path—they were free to discover their own passions. Instead, she wanted them to feel a deep sense of responsibility to do as well as they could and to be generous of spirit. There was a certain firmness in Ann's voice when she declared that she expected her kids to do their best.

Ann exemplified the values she was trying to teach by resolutely continuing to study, work, and pursue a career in areas that inspired her. This involved connecting with a wide range of people and focusing on the welfare of others. In this she was helped by her parents, especially her mother.

Well before the Oscar-winning *Guess Who's Coming to Dinner* made its debut, Ann startled her parents by her choice of partners. But far from judging or rejecting her daughter, Ann's mother provided unconditional love and support, especially in looking after Ann's son when he was studying in America.

So how did Ann's kids turn out? Rather well. After completing two masters degrees and her PhD, Maya became a high school and college teacher. And Ann's son, Barack, went on to become the forty-fourth president of the United States.

Barack Obama has been able to bring together the diverse elements of his background to unite a vast array of people around the world. Some key elements of Ann shone through in his moving inauguration speech. He displayed her sense of compassion that was always blended with determination and toughness.

Above all, Ann showed how a parent who lived an inspired life, provided unconditional love, and developed a sense of care and responsibility in her children could help them overcome any obstacles to realizing their dreams and making a difference.

Lessons from Life: Arun's Own Story

A disrupted family life, indifferent school record, lack of business skills, and being shy do not sound like the ingredients for launching an ambitious entrepreneurial career. Nevertheless, twenty-five years later, the company I helped to launch has been remarkably successful and my life journey has been one of personal development and considerable fulfilment.

When I reflect on my personal journey and some of the lessons I am trying to pass on to my two sons, ages thirteen and ten, these are some of the most important.

- I benefited hugely from my parents' love of learning and exposure to different ideas, cultures, and people. My mother, a teacher, was passionate about educating children, classical dancing, and cooking, and she shared my father's interest in world affairs. She was also one of the most generous and loving people I have ever known. My father had been groomed to inherit a successful family business, but he discovered a love of journalism so great that, as he approaches his eightieth birthday, he remains an active writer.

- Despite their own troubled marriage, there was not a single day when I doubted my parents would love me regardless of my career, my partner, or my beliefs. My mother's only aspiration for me was that I would grow up to be a decent, caring person, and that I would be happy.

- My parents gave me the self-confidence to follow my own path. My background involved moving between countries and cities; I ended up going to seven different schools. All of those changes were crucial, however, in giving me the confidence to follow my dreams.

- My parents were well educated but poorly paid, and they had no financial or business skills. Money was very limited, which led me to work part-time in supermarkets as soon as I was old enough. I learned from my parents that the sources of inspiration evolve and change, and it is easy to develop new skills when one is truly inspired.

- The turning point in my academic life occurred in high school, where I was blessed with teachers who brought their subjects to life, especially economics and history. Because of them, all of a sudden I loved schoolwork, and to the surprise of everyone, including myself, I graduated among the top students.

- My mother and father viewed new challenges as an important part of enjoying life's journey. After three years in academia, I discovered that being a thinker was not enough. I wanted to be a doer. It was unclear how my work at the university was going to make a real difference to people in poor countries. Academic life offered no security of tenure or income—and coming from a childhood where money was scarce, security was important to me.

- Making a significant amount of money has greatly increased my sense of financial security, given me a sense of independence, and increased my well-being.

- Having the ability to establish a family foundation that focuses on providing microfinance to poor entrepreneurs and the education of children from disadvantaged backgrounds has enriched me. I plan to spend more time on these for the rest of my life. Being able to enjoy a few more luxuries has been pleasant, but this has had little or no enduring effect on my sense of well-being.

- The strong relationships among the ipac securities founders—Paul Clitheroe, Suvan de Soysa, Peeyush Gupta, and me—who remain together after twenty five years, are friendships that will last a lifetime. Also precious have been the relationships built with many of my colleagues, not least with my coauthor, Andrew Ford, and with clients who have given us the privilege of guiding their life plans, in some cases for more than twenty years.

We face increasing pressures to be perfect parents and to produce perfect kids. Yet our child-centric societies, with their array of daunting and demanding child-rearing prescriptions, are not producing more children who display emotional resilience and sound money behaviors.

Parents should consider taking a more relaxed, simple, and realistic approach that focuses on their children's well-being. There is no need to micromanage our children's lives or to direct their careers, marriage partners, or beliefs. First and foremost is to provide our children with unconditional love to give them the confidence to think for themselves and pursue their interests. Second is to expose them to a variety of experiences, including those that we are passionate about, to help them discover what inspires them. Third is to develop a sense of responsibility and core values.

With this approach, our children are likely to consistently surprise us as to how they creatively connect the dots of their various passions and competences to lead fulfilling lives, and to overcome inevitable failures along the way.

Last but not least is to develop in our children a spirit of generosity—to learn the deeper sources of happiness that come from giving with meaning, which we explore in the next chapter.

Chapter 6

GIVING WITH MEANING

THIS CHINESE PROVERB CAPTURES THE VERY REAL BENEFIT to us of providing help to another person:

> If you want to be happy
> ... for an hour, take a nap.
> ... for a day, go fishing.
> ... for a month, get married.
> ... for a year, get an inheritance.
> ... for a lifetime, help someone.

The author Gore Vidal, a noted wit and social critic, once commented, "Every time a friend succeeds, I die a little." This acerbic comment reflects the stark reality that it kills us a little each time we learn that someone has fared better than we have, has invested more wisely, or simply has been blessed with luck. This negative feeling is a major obstacle to applying the lessons in this book. So, what causes it, and how can we develop a more generous spirit?

Generosity is part of our evolutionary inheritance. We know that cooperating within the tribe enhanced our survival; a degree of generosity brought an evolutionary advantage. However, there was a limit to generosity. On no account could it lead to the tribe advancing ahead of the individual, because that would mean certain death.

Gore Vidal's reference to friends is insightful because the success of people who are distant from us matters little. It's our peer group that affects us: will the success of our siblings or best friends cause them to leave us behind?

While these limitations on generosity made sense in the past, we now have the opportunity to overcome envy to enhance both our own happiness and that of those around us. Perhaps the ultimate prize is to move from a life that is successful for you to a life that is also meaningful to others. If you make a difference to just one person, the impact on the well-being of both of you can be similar to those whose reach extends to millions. As Winston Churchill said, "We make a living by what we get; we make a life by what we give."

The rest of this chapter is devoted to stories of people who are giving, whether it involves time or money or both. Their motives vary widely, from a caring spirit, to a positive response, to a sense of injustice, to a personal tragedy. What is important in these examples is that the givers are doing so not in order to make themselves happy, but with a sense of inspiration and empathy.

REFLECTIONS: How much time did you spend helping others in the past two weeks? In the past three months? In the past twelve months? Were those times when you helped others rewarding for them? Were they rewarding for you?

THE GROCER WITH THE BROADEST GRIN

The most direct way to make a difference in someone's life is to commit your personal time and effort, without expectation of recognition or reward. Most parents instinctively do this with their children, but journalist Greg Bearup's story of Geoffrey Lee and Bilel Jideh shows that such relationships can extend beyond family.

Geoffrey Lee immigrated to Australia from China when he was twelve. He worked in his uncle's fruit shop while putting himself through school. After years of hard work, Lee was able to buy his own grocery store and café. He employed three or four children after school. They came from poor migrant families and would earn a little money by washing dishes, peeling potatoes, or sweeping floors.

Geoffrey's own education had been hampered by poor English skills. When things were quiet in the store, he would encourage the children working for him by helping with their homework.

Bilel Jideh, the son of Lebanese immigrants, had poor communication skills when he began working for Lee. At home he spoke only Arabic, and Lee could not get him to read. Bilel was nearly last in every subject at school. While expecting that the best Bilel could hope for would be an apprenticeship, Lee nonetheless consistently encouraged the boy to study.

The turning point for Bilel came when one of Lee's daughters topped the state in two subjects and went on to study medicine. Inspired, Bilel told Lee that he, too, wanted to study medicine. His mentor pointed out that this would involve reading many, many books. Slowly Bilel began to read. A page a day at first soon became several, then ten, and eventually more than a hundred. He spent long evenings and weekends in the shop, studying.

By the end of his freshman year in high school, Bilel had won a prize for most improved student. In his final year, he topped every subject and was valedictorian of his class. He narrowly missed qualifying for medicine, but he went on to complete a medical science degree with distinction. Thereafter, he was accepted to med school, and he began the further long years of study to qualify as a doctor.

Reflecting on his considerable progress toward achieving what once seemed like an impossible dream, Bilel says, "I could not have achieved any of it without Geoff. He showed me the way. My parents were so proud. I am the first from my entire extended family to go to university. You should have seen the feasts here, and in Lebanon!"

The beauty of Lee's generosity is that he provided the shoulders upon which Bilel could stand in order to attain a degree of success that far exceeded anything he would otherwise have known.

And Lee's reward? "He was just as proud," says Bilel. "He couldn't stop grinning for days."

OAKS FROM ACORNS

Muhammad Yunus learned the importance of education from his father, and compassion from his mother, who would help any poor person who knocked on their door. Muhammad won a Fulbright Scholarship, which enabled him to complete a doctorate in economics and teach in the United States, before returning home to Bangladesh. It was 1974, and times were grim. The country had just won independence in a bloody war with Pakistan, but it was stricken by famine.

"We middle class people tried to ignore it," Dr. Yunus later wrote, "but then skeleton-like people began showing up in the capital, Dhaka. Soon the trickle became a flood. Hungry people were everywhere. Often they sat so still that one could not be sure whether they were alive or dead."

Although Yunus wanted to help, he had no idea where to start. He began to visit villages to understand the struggles of the poor firsthand. In Jobra, he met a young mother, Sufiya Begum, who made bamboo stools. She would do this squatting on the hard mud in her front yard while at the same time keeping an eye on her three children.

The bamboo to make a stool cost just 22 cents, but Sufiya had to borrow this from middlemen, who then forced her to sell the stools to them at a discount, leaving her an income of just 2 cents a day. This barely fed her family.

Sufiya could have borrowed money from the moneylenders in her village, but interest rates started at around 500 percent annually, and could go as high as 5,000 percent. Back in his economics department, Professor Yunus had theorized about the investment of millions of dollars. He found himself shocked and angry that he and others in his profession had failed to address problems of life and death like Sufiya's, which involved only a few cents. He could see that the existing economic system condemned her, along with her children and grandchildren, to a life of penury.

Yunus decided to act immediately. He made a list of all the people in the village who were dependent on middlemen for tiny amounts of money. He was stunned to find that the total borrowed was merely $27. He decided to lend this amount to the villagers, to be repaid when they could afford it.

The lives of those he helped were transformed. The impact on their well-being was so great, and their commitment to repaying the loans so strong, that Yunus approached major banks to expand the program. But these banks could not see beyond the illiteracy of the villagers. "They can't fill out our forms," they told Yunus. They also emphasized the lack of available collateral and alleged lack of honesty. "Those people will never pay back the loans," they said.

After many trials and setbacks, Yunus established the Grameen (Village) Bank, focused entirely on lending to the poor. What started as a homegrown project, run with the help of some of Professor Yunus's students, has now loaned more than $6 billion to nearly 7 million poor villagers, 97 percent of whom are women.

The bank provides loans for small enterprises and for students. It also provides collateral-free loans for housing. The typical loan is under $100.

The loan repayment rate is 99 percent. These small loans have allowed some 58 percent of borrowers to cross the poverty line. In Bangladesh about 80 percent of poor families have now been reached by microcredit. Many more of the children go to school. The Grameen Bank makes seven thousand new student loans each year and awards thirty thousand scholarships. The cycle of poverty for many of these families has ended.

Yunus emphasizes that Grameen Bank needs to charge interest and make a profit, while ensuring that loans are affordable. He defines his work as a business with a social objective: to get people out of poverty. Rather than providing a return to investors, profits are ploughed back into the bank to keep increasing the reach of its programs.

Today, thousands of other microcredit programs operate around the world, inspired by the Grameen Bank model. It is probably the most innovative and important development in the fight against poverty of the past one hundred years. In 2006 Muhammad Yunus was awarded the Nobel Peace Prize for his work. But recognition was not his motivation. The Grameen Bank grew out of his feelings of helplessness. Dismayed by the famine and poverty around him, Yunus had a simple thought. "As a human being, I can go out and help another person."

"WHAT HAVE I GOT TO LOSE?"

In 1949, David Bussau was abandoned at the age of nine to the care of a New Zealand orphanage. Life at the Boys' Home was tough, both emotionally and physically, but in spite of this, he developed tenacity and opportunism. To him, failure wasn't a big deal. His attitude was, "What do I have to lose?" This mind-set, together with his incredible work ethic, led him to his first entrepreneurial venture at the age of sixteen. He rented a hot dog stand. It thrived.

That was only the beginning. In 1975, he was the wealthy owner of a number of successful construction companies in Sydney, Australia, but for the young Bussau, material success felt hollow. When Cyclone Tracy devastated the city of Darwin, he was at a crossroads in his life. Immediately upon hearing about what had happened, he rounded up a team of volunteers who spent three weeks rushing from house to house in the disaster area doing repairs. Bussau was exhilarated by the challenging and satisfying work.

Yet he was worried about an element of selfishness in what he had done. "Is it really about me helping people, or is it about me feeling good about myself?" he wondered. (In later years, when he sat back to reflect on this period, he labeled it as having reached the "economics of enough.") He was at a turning point: he could decide to pursue great wealth, or he could take the more modest success and wealth he had and employ them for social benefit.

Bussau made a further commitment. He decided to disband the business interests he had built up. He moved his young family to Darwin to take over the coordination of the rebuilding program.

Two years later he got a call to help a community in Bali, which did not have the money to rebuild its small village after a destructive earthquake. Bussau knew it would be costly to have to pay for the building materials and support his family in Bali for as long as it would take to put the village back together again. He welcomed the challenge, however, and saw it as a true exercise in faith.

During his years in Bali, his perception of poverty was recast. He realized that the causes were complex and even endemic. What he found most distressing was the loss of hope and sense of futility felt by the poor

Balinese when faced with such a huge task. Entire families were locked into generational debt, with no hope for the children to escape a life of hard labor. Over them hung the specter of moneylenders waiting to profit from their need.

Bussau's entrepreneurial brain took over. He knew the answer lay in getting the community to help itself. If he could loan some money to local people with good business ideas, work could be generated for other people in the village. And so the concept of microfinance in Bali was born at about the same time that Muhammad Yunus was beginning his miracle bank in Bangladesh.

Back in Australia, Bussau and his family decided to move ahead with the development work they had started in Indonesia. Within two years, they had sold and transferred all their assets, other than their family home, into their private philanthropic trust, Maranatha. After Bali, they knew how happy they could be with a simple lifestyle. They didn't yearn for vacation houses and expensive clothes. They decided to invest their money, skills, and talent in this work, their calling. It would be more than a job or an act of altruism. It would become a way of life. There was no going back.

This would ultimately lead to the cofounding of Opportunity International in 1979, whose foundation is built on the simple truth that many of the world's poorest people are a good credit risk. A lifetime of struggling for food and shelter fosters the kind of single-minded drive that it takes to start and build a small business. Rather than staying victims, the world's poor can engineer their own emergence from poverty. Given a working chance, they can begin to build brighter futures. As income increases, businesses are able to expand, and the effect spreads beyond the family into the community, through employment and contributions to the local economy. The benefits of microfinance and enterprise development help build stronger communities.

In 2006 Opportunity International lent more than $400 million in nearly a million loans. More than 85 percent of the loans went to women, and the on-time repayment rate was 98 percent. The organization's reach is rapidly expanding. It is estimated that more than 10 million men, women, and children have benefited from its global programs. In recognition of its work

Opportunity International has received more than $17 million from the Bill & Melinda Gates Foundation to help fund its expansion in Africa.

Had Bussau not asked himself "how much is enough?" at the age of thirty-five, he might never have embarked on a new path that would benefit millions of other people. He made a decision and never looked back—and has never been happier.

You can find out more about Opportunity International by visiting its website at www.opportunity.org.

THE NEW AMERICAN DREAM

Dick and Patty Simon live in a suburb of Boston, and at first glance they appear to be a typical middle-class American family. Dick owns a real estate company and Patty is an artist. Their three children still live at home and attend school. But here the similarity ends. In August 1999, they embarked upon a journey that would change their lives.

Dick and Patty had gone backpacking around the world for a year in 1985. Now it was time to take to the road again with their three young children—Alex, age ten, Katie, eight, and Ben, six. This suburban family closed up their businesses, organized home-schooling kits, and left their home comforts for adventures in Costa Rica, Guatemala, Honduras, Thailand, Laos, Cambodia, India, Nepal, Bhutan, Japan, China, Botswana, Namibia, Tanzania, and Europe for nine months.

Patty described the wonder of seeing the world through the eyes of their children. But the couple's real hope was that they would come back with a broader perspective, an understanding that having the latest electronic game was not the biggest deal, together with a sense of wanting to make a difference. Whereas most parents agonize over how to protect their kids from the realities of the world, Dick and Patty's attitude was "bring it on!"

After returning from the trip, Alex started a microcredit club at his school, raising awareness about what it is and fundraising through the sale of Guatemalan handicrafts, as well as home-baked goods and candy. The club then loaned all the funds raised to microentrepreneurs around the world. Two years ago, at sixteen, Alex cofounded Youth Microcredit

International (www.ymci.org), following in the footsteps of Yunus and Bussau. It provides microloans to small business owners in developing countries. The organization has numerous chapters around the world. Alex has made frequent trips to Guatemala to educate young people about microloan borrowing and to cultivate relationships with borrowers. YMCI has facilitated, raised, and loaned more than $40,000 to date.

Alex is also the Massachusetts representative of a program to create the first public university dedicated to public service. He cofounded the Kids with Cameras program, which gives children living in the Guatemala City dump area the opportunity to express themselves through photography. Alex has visited more than forty-five countries, predominantly in the developing world, to explore cultural and socioeconomic issues.

The nine-month family trip also had a profound effect on Katie. At age seven, she says, she met kids her own age who faced problems to which she would never be exposed: illiteracy, malnutrition, poverty. Two years ago at a summer leadership camp she learned about the international sex trade in children. More than 2 million children, some as young as four, are being exploited. Child prostitutes can be forced to service more than twenty-five customers per day and are at extreme risk of contracting HIV. Hundreds of thousands of young girls and boys are abused in the multibillion-dollar child pornography and human-trafficking industries. "Sex tours" are arranged for tourists (25 percent of whom are American) traveling with the specific purpose of having sex with minors.

Katie learned about a rehabilitation center for child prostitutes in the Philippines and organized a yard sale with her friends. Her goal was to raise $5,000 to support the project. She raised more than $6,500 and, importantly, found that she enjoyed making a difference. She was having fun and felt good about it.

Katie founded the organization Minga (www.mingagroup.org) to do more. Its mission is to support and create programs directly benefiting victims of the child sex trade; to educate others about this problem and empower them to take action; and to advocate for and enforce preventative measures against the horrific cycle of exploitation. In the Quechua language, *minga* means the coming together of the community for the collective good.

Since Minga was founded in August 2006, the group has raised more than $51,000 for the rehabilitation center in the Philippines. Katie led a group of a dozen Minga members on a trip to Guatemala, where they met with children living on the street. They also met with local organizations with which they could form partnerships to donate much-needed school and art supplies. A meeting they had with a twelve-year-old mother and her baby had an especially strong impact on the American teenagers. They returned home and shared these stories with their peers, encouraging action in dozens of schools in the area.

Minga is also working with American Airlines and others to show a short in-flight video about child sex tourism, warning potential exploiters that they are legally as accountable for their abuses internationally as they are in their home countries.

Katie says that the impact of what she is doing is twofold. On one level she is helping the victims of horrific abuse; on another level she is creating powerful waves of social awareness and change in her own community. She is helping affluent American teenagers look at their lives in a different way and in so doing giving them a whole new take on the words "giving with meaning."

And let's not forget Ben. At age thirteen he started Simon Lawn Care, which, he says, is the cheapest lawn-mowing service in his suburb and definitely the most successful. The reason is that his neighbors support him because they know half of his earnings go to support worthy microfinance ventures.

As they set out nine years ago, Patty and Dick could never have envisaged the ways in which the minds of their young children would be opened to the world. Now there is no happier place for them to be than around their dinner table at night, listening to their children debating the merits of microfinance over intervention in the child sex trade.

COMMITTED TO A CURE

Can the death of a child inspire someone to devote the rest of his or her life to others? In an extraordinary number of cases, this has indeed happened. One of the most remarkable stories is that of Dr. Susan Alberti.

After growing up in Melbourne, Australia, Danielle Alberti, Susan's daughter, took on the challenge of living in New York, and like most young people, enjoyed herself there. However, most are not also diagnosed with juvenile diabetes at a young age, as Danielle had been, nor do they suffer the pain of their father having been killed in an accident. The disease started to take a severe toll on the young woman's health.

Dr. Alberti flew to New York and found her daughter seriously ill. She had planned for an emergency mother-daughter kidney transplant in Australia, but on the flight home, Danielle died. Can any of us really imagine what Susan Alberti must have felt during that nine-hour flight? Not a day goes by without her recalling that trip home, she says.

She could have retreated into grief. Instead, the tragedy inspired Dr. Alberti to act with fierce determination. She had already been president for five years of the Juvenile Diabetes Research Foundation (JDRF), juggling its demands with her professional life. After Danielle's death, she vowed to redouble her efforts to conquer the disease. In addition to contributing $5 million herself, she has spearheaded a fund-raising drive that raised a further $20 million. She has worked tirelessly to help coordinate global research efforts and raise awareness of the disease.

In 2006, Susan Alberti herself was diagnosed with both latent juvenile diabetes and Hodgkin's lymphoma. Her determination was undiminished, however, and later that year she led a delegation of a hundred children with juvenile diabetes to Australia's Parliament House to promote JDRF's cause.

All of us will have been touched, directly or indirectly, by a serious disease attacking a loved one, and many will want to contribute to medical research as a result. But how do we know whether the organization to which we are contributing uses our money well? The approach of JDRF is instructive to those with such an interest.

Stephen Higgs, JDRF's director, who was inspired by his own son's illness and Dr. Alberti's passion, explains that as an organization with a relatively modest budget, it is essential for JDRF to use research dollars wisely. The organization acts like the conductor of an orchestra. It tries to coordinate the work of many individual scientists, medical research organizations, and drug companies. It wants to sponsor research that is innovative and likely to make a difference, rather than wasting money on duplicating studies that have already proved unsuccessful elsewhere.

This approach has produced valuable breakthroughs. Through its international affiliations, JDRF has inspired NASA and the Department of Defense in the United States to undertake research on maintaining blood-sugar levels, an important issue for astronauts and for soldiers operating under stress in the field. This research is likely to lead to much less painful ways of testing blood-sugar levels, and to the development of a pump that automatically injects the right amount of insulin into diabetes sufferers.

Significant progress has also been made in the transplant of tiny islets that secrete insulin into the pancreas. Cooperation with researchers in the better-established fields of heart and kidney transplants has meant more effective therapies are being used.

In her leading role in JDRF over a long period, Susan Alberti provides a powerful example of how a passionate commitment to helping others can provide the spiritual and emotional energy to overcome the most devastating personal tragedy. As Higgs observes, "She has bounced back with more determination from every setback. She has inspired us all by showing that she will never give up."

THE $30 BILLION MAN

When Microsoft cofounder Bill Gates read an article about diseases in the developing world, he learned that every year, malaria kills a million people, most of them children in Africa under the age of five.

Gates decided to find out more. But the more he read, the less he liked what he learned. He found out that millions of children were also dying each year from other diseases that had been eliminated years ago in the United States. Tuberculosis, for instance, remained endemic in the developing world. Some diseases, such as rotavirus, he had never even heard of.

Until reading about these diseases Gates and his wife, Melinda, had assumed that governments were doing everything they could to get vaccines and treatments to people who desperately needed them. But what they discovered shocked them.

"We couldn't escape the brutal conclusion that in our world today some lives are seen as worth saving and others are not," Gates said in an address to the World Health Assembly in Geneva in 2005.

Gates, then the world's richest person, decided to do something about it. He and his wife are now in the process of donating tens of billions of dollars of their personal wealth to organizations that are addressing some of the world's most intractable health problems.

The Bill & Melinda Gates Foundation has a bigger welfare program than many governments. With more than $30 billion in its coffers, it is addressing problems ranging from the global malaria and AIDS epidemics to public libraries and the United States high school system, which Gates calls "obsolete."

It now funds more than one-third of global malaria research. Scientists working for it have been able to manufacture the most effective drug to treat the disease, previously in short supply. The cost to save a life is expected to fall from $2.40 to 25 cents per dose.

Some cynics may think that Gates is merely seeking to preserve his name, or that this is the least someone with tens of billions of dollars can do for the world. The important thing, though, is that what is inspiring Gates is a genuine sense of injustice and desire to make a difference. How many of the world's wealthy people, including the middle classes of the developed world, would consider giving away more than one-third of their wealth to improve the lives of strangers?

What values underpin the causes that the foundation has chosen to support? Understanding their approach to this question is interesting for anyone considering philanthropy, even if our budgets are only a small fraction of the Gates's.

The foundation decided to focus its initial efforts on where it believed it could make the biggest difference to people's lives. The current focus on global health and the American high school system enables it to learn about the best approaches in each area and thus to have the greatest possible impact, its founders say. Says Gates:

> Every day, more than 1,000 children die because they didn't get a 15-cent measles vaccine. Almost 3 billion

> people around the world live on less than $2 per day. Here in the United States, only one-third of the students who start in the ninth grade will graduate from high school with the skills they need to succeed in college and work. A disproportionate number of those who fall behind will be African-American and Hispanic.
>
> Our foundation and our partners are trying to solve these problems because we believe that all lives have equal value, no matter where they are being lived.

Despite the enormity of the challenges he has set for his foundation, Gates remains optimistic. "We have a chance to make sure that all people, no matter what country they live in, will have the preventive care, vaccines, and treatments they need to live a healthy life. I believe we can do this. And if we do, it will be the best thing humanity has ever done."

The Gates's approach has been so inspiring that in June 2006, the foundation's efforts received a huge boost, with fellow billionaire and Bill Gates's mentor, Warren Buffett, announcing his intention to contribute 85 percent of his personal fortune to it.

We hope these stories have inspired you to start thinking about how your signature strengths can be turned toward benefiting the lives of others. Balancing wealth and well-being for ourselves and deciding how much is enough are important, but each of us also has the power to influence the lives of those around us. We can do this every day: often in small ways, sometimes more momentously. How we choose to use our power for good helps define our humanity and give meaning to our own life and the lives of others.

PUTTING IT INTO PRACTICE

So where do you start? Giving money to charities, while a good thing to do, will not be the magic ingredient. First is to try and build giving into the way you make a living. If you are in one of the caring professions, such as teaching or nursing, you are off to a good start. However, professions such as investment banking, commercial law, and business strategy also offer opportunities for individuals to apply their considerable skills to help others—for example, through pro bono projects.

Generosity will work best if your desire to give is sparked by a sense of inspiration, not obligation. A useful way to explore this is to think of those things for which you feel a strong sense of gratitude, that offer inspiration, or that demonstrate injustice.

Here's a personal example. When the first edition of this book was published, the authors reflected on how grateful we were that our respective children went to schools where teachers helped them learn *how* to think, rather than *what* to think. One of us decided to take his children to school the next morning, give each of their teachers a copy of this book, and express some words of gratitude for their work. The teachers were at first apprehensive, and then surprised to receive a gift. Whether this made them happy, we simply don't know. But the giver experienced a good feeling that lasted for weeks, even though the value of the gift was so small. It highlighted how rewarding giving with meaning can be when the motives are genuine.

In turn this led us to donate time to helping teachers of schools we have attended to convey to students some of the lessons of this book. It has also led us to work with a charity, The Smith Family, whose focus is the education of children from disadvantaged backgrounds.

Try a few experiments for yourself. What better time to start than when giving a birthday, anniversary, or holiday gift to someone who "has everything"?

Think of a present that you have bought for your partner or someone close to you and write down, out of a possible 10 points, how happy buying that present has made you and how happy you think it made the recipient.

Next, write down how happy gifting money to a charity in the name of your partner will make you and him or her, respectively.

Then, visit the website www.kiva.org, the eBay of microfinance, where you can change the life of a poor entrepreneur in a developing country for as little as $25. The website works in conjunction with sixty-seven microfinance institutions around the world that recommend the borrowers and administer the loans. The process is amazingly simple—you browse the profiles of potential borrowers, find one you like, and pay via PayPal. You can do interesting things like buy a poor family in Azerbaijan a goat or help a baker set up shop in Cambodia. Make these gifts in the name of your partner. Once the loans are set up, your partner will receive regular repayments, usually monthly, until the loan is paid off, as well as regular updates on how the recipient is faring. The repayment rate on these loans is a staggering 99 percent.

When the loan has been repaid, your partner can do what he or she wishes with the money, but don't be surprised if the money gets loaned to another entrepreneur and the cycle starts all over again. The beauty of kiva is that it is a peer-to-peer transaction, which means that all your money reaches the recipient. Compare this with some of the bigger charities where 30 percent of the money gets eaten up on overhead.

When you tell your partner about the gift in his or her name, bring its value to life. Share with your partner or friend what the life of the recipients is like and what a difference the gift will make. The fact is that the poor do not need pity; they need opportunity.

Now ask your partner to rate how happy this gift has made him or her and also rate it yourself. Compare it to the rating that each of you gave your material gift.

Most people who have tried this experiment do not expect it to do much for their happiness or that of their partner. However, as they go through the exercise, their perception changes. A month after the gift is given, both parties invariably report higher well-being from the choice of this gift than a material item. By becoming more generous of spirit, you can increase the well-being of the people around you as well as your own. It is one of the best investments in yourself and others that you can make.

The exercise above can work with kids as well. We recommend that you ritualize this exercise with your children at their birthdays and at Christmas. Introduce them to the idea that to mark how special these occasions are, it is appropriate to give as well as to receive.

Here is something we have tried with our children and with high school students. Give your children some money to buy for themselves whatever they want to spend the money on. Give them the same amount of money to spend on the kiva site (or any other charity they want to support). Finally, encourage your children to write a letter of gratitude which they present and read out to someone that *they* feel has played an important role in their lives.

These latter two activities will work best if the child is encouraged rather than coerced into doing them. It will help the children if they think about what or whom has inspired them or what they feel a sense of gratitude for. The letter of gratitude needs to be more than a thank-you note. Tal Ben-Shahar describes the ideal letter as a thoughtful examination of the meaning and pleasure that one derives from the relationship; it describes particular experiences and shared dreams and whatever else in the relationship is a source of joy.

Ask your children to rate their happiness at the time of doing each of these things and then a week later. Invariably, they will discover, if doing the exercise for the first time, that the letter of gratitude has the greatest impact. We have found that teenagers will present these letters to friends at school. They initially feel shy about doing this, and boys in particular are not sure what reaction they will get from their friends. But the turning point is discovering how great the delight of the recipients is and how the bonds of friendship are greatly strengthened. These children have discovered the joy in Buddha's insight that "thousands of candles can be lighted from a single candle, and the life of the candle will not be shortened. Happiness never decreases by being shared."

The generosity of spirit that can come from truly understanding this insight and from reaping the benefits of giving with meaning can yield this result: the next time a friend succeeds, any sense of envy will be replaced by real joy.

Do you have an inspiring story of someone who is giving with meaning that you would like us to know about? Please visit our website at www. howmuchisenough.net and share it with us.

FURTHER READING FOR PART 1

WE HIGHLY RECOMMEND THE FOLLOWING BOOKS if you are interested in further exploring the issues discussed in chapters 1 through 6.

Tal Ben-Shahar's *Happier: Learn the Secrets to Daily Joy and Lasting Fulfillment* is a beautifully written book that blends positive psychology with philosophy and practical exercises.

Stephanie Dowrick's *Choosing Happiness: Life and Soul Essentials* combines depth, practicality, and lightness in exploring the paths to happiness.

Linda and Richard Eyre's *Teaching Your Children Responsibility* provides a good framework and lots of practical advice for rearing socially and financially responsible children.

Tim Kasser's *The High Price of Materialism* is helpful in developing a well-balanced set of values and challenging the excessive role materialism can unconsciously play in our lives.

Scott Pape's *The Barefoot Investor: Five Steps to Financial Freedom* is a very accessible investment guide for older teens and young adults.

Matthieu Ricard's *Happiness: A Guide to Developing Life's Most Important Skill* is a lyrical book for those seeking spiritual depth and valuable meditative exercises.

Martin Seligman's *Authentic Happiness: Using the New Positive Psychology to Realize Your Potential for Lasting Fulfillment* was the groundbreaking book in positive psychology.

Tim Sharp's *The Happiness Handbook: Strategies for a Happy Life* has many practical exercises that are being used with success by thousands who have attended his coaching clinics.

PART 2

WEALTH HABITS:

Practical ways to enhance your wealth and overcome
"thought traps" that prevent this from happening

Chapter 7

THE INVESTMENT PRIZE

NEVER BEFORE HAVE WE BEEN BLESSED with such a range of investment opportunities and the potential to achieve financial independence. Using these opportunities well is the key to developing a successful investment strategy, the third pillar of our Bridge of Well-being.

There are endless ways to invest and make money, from riding the property cycle, to holding bonds and cash, to building your own business. All these have a role to play in wealth creation. Many of them may produce good results. In the short term, as was amply demonstrated during the financial crisis of 2008, the stock market can be like a roller coaster that occasionally subjects investors to hair-raising plunges. Nevertheless, for most people, investing in the stock market offers the best and most accessible opportunity to create personal wealth over the long haul, as part owner of a range of businesses. The idea is simple: rather than putting money in the bank, why not own part of the bank?

What's important to long-term investment success is adhering to the principles of Quality, Value, Diversity, and Time that we introduced in chapter 1 and explain in more detail in chapter 11.

If it's relatively easy to acquire a diversified portfolio of stocks, set long-term goals, and develop a plan and stick to it over time, why do so few succeed when so many others of equal or even greater ability fail? The great economist and successful investor John Maynard Keynes provided part of the answer when he commented, "Investors may be quite willing to take the risk of being wrong in the company of others, while being much more reluctant to take the risk of being right alone." For our prehistoric ancestors, being one of the herd was necessary for survival, but in today's world it is not. In short, Keynes blamed most people's failure in investment markets on the herd mentality, a form of peer pressure or conformity applied to the markets.

The stock market is also a complex environment, and the human brain is not well equipped to make sense of it all. Our emotions and biases can easily destroy our wealth.

Because harnessing the power of stock markets is critical to long-term financial success, investors must overcome those obstacles.

Perhaps the single most powerful observation about the performance of investment markets, an insight that can make the most difference to long-term financial success, is that on average, over long periods of time, shares have outperformed cash and fixed interest investments by around 5–7 percent annually. This has certainly not happened every year, nor even over every five-year period. But, on average, it has held true.

In the past century, shares produced higher returns than the risk-free cash rate in every major market including all ten-year periods in the United States since 1939 and every twenty- and thirty-year period in that market. The table on the following page shows the consistent and significant outperformance of shares over fixed interest investments, after taking into account the inflation rate, in every major market during the twentieth century. The Australian stock market produced the strongest returns of all, with a huge 6.6 percent gap in annualized returns between shares and bonds. Even in Switzerland, where the gap between returns from shares and bonds was smallest, the stock market still outstripped bonds by an average of 1.9 percent per annum.

While no one can predict the future, barring extreme events, this basic relationship should continue to hold true. The return above the cash rate from shares is called the equity risk premium, but we'll call it the Investment Prize. It is one of a handful of resilient forces in the world of investing.

Capturing the Investment Prize as part of your wealth creation strategy can make the difference between a lifestyle that meets your expectations— now and in the future—and a lifestyle in which you just get by. When

Real returns on shares compared with bonds internationally, 1900–2007

	Shares (%)	Bonds (%)
Belgium	2.5	–0.2
Italy	2.5	–1.8
Germany	3.4	–1.8
France	3.7	–0.3
Spain	4.0	1.3
Japan	4.3	–1.3
Norway	4.5	1.6
Switzerland	4.5	2.6
Ireland	4.6	1.0
Denmark	5.3	3.0
World ex United States	5.3	1.2
Netherlands	5.4	1.3
United Kingdom	5.5	1.3
World	5.8	1.7
Canada	6.3	2.0
United States	6.5	1.9
South Africa	7.5	1.7
Sweden	7.8	2.4
Australia	7.9	1.3

Source: ABN/AMRO/LBS, Global Investment Returns Yearbook 2008, Chart 14

you're making choices about the timing of your retirement, the lifestyle you can afford, and the options available to you, it can help stack the odds in your favor.

Over the average investment lifetime of around thirty years, that extra 5–7 percent per annum makes a remarkable difference to your retirement capital, thanks to the power of markets and the benefit of compounding returns.

HOW TO MAKE A MILLION DOLLARS

Say you invest $100,000 today and receive a 4 percent return each year for thirty years, compounded monthly. Ignoring inflation and taxes, and assuming you reinvest all income, after thirty years you have $331,350. Not bad.

Now, say you invest the same $100,000 over the same thirty-year period, but this time your average return is 5 percent higher, the lower end of the historical range of the equity risk premium in the United States. After thirty years you come away with $1,473,057—a difference of more than a million dollars! Suddenly, retirement is a much brighter proposition. Your ability to make the most of life's choices has been dramatically enhanced.

The Investment Prize Is Enduring

The encouraging news is that, despite periods when the Investment Prize seems to disappear—notable examples are the Depression of the 1930s, the plunge in world stock markets between 2000 and 2003, and the bear market of 2007 and 2008 prompted by a shakeout in the subprime mortgage market in the United States—there are good reasons for it to return, and it always has.

Theory says that investors must be compensated, over time, for the higher risk of owning shares, compared with cash or bonds. Without the expectation of extra returns, there would be no reason for anyone to own shares. So, quite simply, no one would.

Theory aside, there's also a simpler practical reason.

Companies Create Wealth

In a market-based economy, wealth is mostly generated through companies. Employees and the self-employed are paid by companies, which sell things to other companies or to consumers. Where do consumers get their spending money? From the companies they work for. Where do they get the money that drives housing booms? From those very same companies.

This highlights why the demand for property is derived from the success of companies. While share and property markets often perform best at different times, a healthy corporate sector ultimately drives a healthy property market, not the other way around.

In a market-based economy, companies that produce lower returns than the interest paid by banks eventually fail. It can take years, but one by one, they are taken over or forced out of business. There's simply no place for them in the market economy.

Only companies that manage to outperform the cash deposit rate survive. By definition, then, the equity risk premium must exist over a long period. Unless you think that global capitalism is about to collapse, quality shares are a sensible place to invest your money.

The Investment Prize is there because of the market system itself. Without it, the system would collapse and the shelves of the investment section at your local bookshop would be empty. In fact, the bookshop would probably not be there at all!

The financial crisis of 2008 exposed some serious flaws in the regulation of the financial sector, which resulted in excessive lending and risk taking on the part of many financial institutions. The unwinding of this caused considerable pain and highlighted a need for tighter regulations. As with previous episodes of financial turbulence, however, the fundamentals underlying the Investment Prize will always remain intact.

YOU ARE IN CHARGE OF YOUR DESTINY

It is true for most people—particularly those planning for retirement— that having sufficient money to support a good lifestyle is a prerequisite for satisfaction and happiness. It is also true that our expectations of the good life have risen faster than our ability to pay for it.

The average retired person now spends more than twenty years, and often up to thirty years, without a salary. Surviving on a low or fixed income— such as a pension or Social Security—has always been a challenge. But we now expect more from retirement, including experiences such as travel, further education, and the opportunity to explore passions and hobbies put on hold during our career and child-rearing phase.

Similarly, many healthcare expenses are no longer regarded as luxuries. Due to breakthroughs in medical science and technology, most people have the opportunity to live longer, healthier lives, with the mapping of the human genome setting off a fresh wave of discovery and possibilities. However, living longer, higher-quality lives comes at a cost.

Who's Going to Pay for Your Future?

The government is not going to pay for your future. Nor the company. Nor your children. The dramatic increase in the proportion of the population age sixty and older means that the growing trend is toward making individuals more and more responsible for funding and investing their retirement savings. Yes, your future is going to be up to you.

As baby boomers enter their fifties and sixties, it is no exaggeration to say that funding retirement is one of the biggest challenges this century in the developed world. With planning and foresight, most people can meet the challenge. Your future lifestyle will depend on how you want to live and how much money you have to finance your lifestyle. Fortunately, you can exert significant control over both. You can determine what's important to you and increase your ability to fund it.

For some, working full-time beyond the traditional retirement age of sixty five is becoming a reality—sometimes forced, but often by choice, too. More common will be a combination of part-time or seasonal work and leisure. Individuals will make choices to suit their circumstances, including their definition of the good life. If your tastes are simple, you'll be happier and more satisfied than someone with loftier aspirations. A good financial adviser can give you a portfolio that is diversified across the asset classes—from shares to property, bonds, and cash—and that at least mirrors the long-term performance of these markets.

Most people think this is the hard part. It's not. All good investment teams can do it, and there are plenty of those. In most cases, however, this is not enough. Despite the emergence of a whole industry providing advice and products, there is no evidence that people are becoming better investors. In fact, the opposite may be true.

The evidence is that the average investor fails to capture the Investment Prize. The difference between success and failure is not how investment markets behave—we know they generally do well over the long term—but how *investors* behave.

IS THE INVESTMENT PRIZE GUARANTEED?

If you want guarantees, it's best to stick to term deposits with major banks. For individuals, capturing the Investment Prize depends on the dates you invest and then withdraw your money. Over short periods, it may not be there at all. It's called a risk premium because you take a risk to get it.

The good news is that the longer your investment time frame, the greater your chances of capturing this extra return.

Extreme events can threaten or remove the premium. Market-based economies may collapse. Germany's did in the 1940s, taking the Investment Prize with it. Risk aversion may fall, so that investors are prepared to take extra risk without anticipating extra return. In this case, the entire equity risk premium could disappear.

A range of different disaster scenarios could unfold, but it's more likely that the Investment Prize will be there for your generation, for your children's generation, and for their children's, too. Betting against it involves betting against a long and convincing history. Despite events such as the U.S. subprime-mortgage-triggered financial crisis, the simple act of investing part of a long-term portfolio in shares, even if you only ever capture the index return and no more, is likely to be one of the most important investment decisions you ever make.

REFLECTIONS: How are your investments allocated now?
When was the last time you checked whether your investment
mix is suitable for your long-term financial success?

What Can Go Wrong?

A formidable body of research shows that investors have often failed to capture the best return from stock markets. The names of these studies say it all: *Manias, Panics and Crashes; Memoirs of Extraordinary Delusions and the Madness of Crowds; The Edge of Chaos: Financial Booms, Bubbles, Crashes, and Chaos;* among numerous others.

In recent years, researchers have sought to measure the underperformance of individual investors versus the markets, with remarkable results.

Not only did most people fail to capture the Investment Prize, but in attempting to do so, average investors achieved lower returns than if they had simply put their money in the bank.

One of the leaders in this area is the independent American investment research group DALBAR Inc., which, since 1994, has been publishing an annual report, *Quantitative Analysis of Investor Behavior.* The subtitle of the report indicates the nature of the research and the findings: *What Investors Really Do, What Is in Their Best Interest, and What It Costs Them.* The 2008 report found that, while the American stock market produced excellent returns in the twenty years to December 31, 2007, the average investor achieved nothing like the return of the market.

While the S&P 500 delivered an annual average return of 11.81 percent for the period, the average investor in share funds in the United States earned just 4.48 percent annually. So investors lost 62 percent of the return available. This was only a little above the return earned by fixed income investors (1.55 percent annually), who themselves earned far less than the return available from a diversified portfolio of bonds. The return that investors achieved from shares was barely higher than the inflation rate over the period.

How did the average American investor miss one of the biggest bull markets in history? Simple. He or she did not buy well-managed funds and hold on to them to achieve double-digit returns similar to the market. Instead, the results suggest that the average investor attempted a market-timing approach, and in so doing, gave up any chance of doing well. In one of history's greatest bull markets, investors seemingly switched in and out of funds at just the wrong time, moving their monies out of low-perform-ing funds *just before* a recovery, and moving into high-performing funds just before a fall.

The DALBAR study supports earlier findings from American research group Morningstar, which surveyed two hundred equity growth funds on their performance for the five years to May 1994. They found their returns averaged 12.5 percent annually.

Morningstar calculated that the average investor's performance over the period was -2.2 percent annually, a remarkable 14.7 percent lower than that of the funds in which they invested.

Only one conclusion is possible: the long-term performance of your investments depends a lot more on how *you* behave than on how *your fund* behaves.

A Brief History of Speculative Disaster

Stock markets are a tough environment in which to make decisions. They are almost the perfect example of a random, chaotic system: complex, uncertain, and full of distractions.

Despite countless billions spent analyzing market trends and performance, not one human alive can tell you for certain how markets will fare this year or next. Before the middle of 2007, when the so-called subprime mortgage crisis emerged in the United States economy, investors were more likely to regard "subprime" as an inferior quality cut of beef than a type of home loan. Who would have thought that a shakeout at the lower-quality end of the mortgage market would lead to a global credit crunch and bring some of the world's major investment houses, such as Bear Stearns, Lehman Brothers, and Merrill Lynch to their knees? Of course, the reaction of many investors throughout both the preceding boom and the eventual shakeout in markets in the second half of 2007 and into 2008 was reassuringly familiar—buy when the market rises, sell when the market falls—and thus they failed to achieve the market return.

The lessons from previous booms and busts have generally not been learned. When the biggest asset price bubble of the modern era, the worldwide technology-stock bubble, peaked in 2000, analysis of cash coming into American equity mutual funds suggests it followed much the same pattern as the South Sea Bubble that ruined Sir Isaac Newton. The most sophisticated, educated, Internet-wise, investment-savvy generation in history had learned nothing from the past.

The chart on the following page shows that inflows into American equity mutual funds leapt to historically high levels as the U.S. stock market rose in 1999 and into early 2000. Net fund flows reached $9 billion in March 2000 and $11 billion the next month. As technology shares began to fall, new investment dried up. It shifted sharply into reverse during

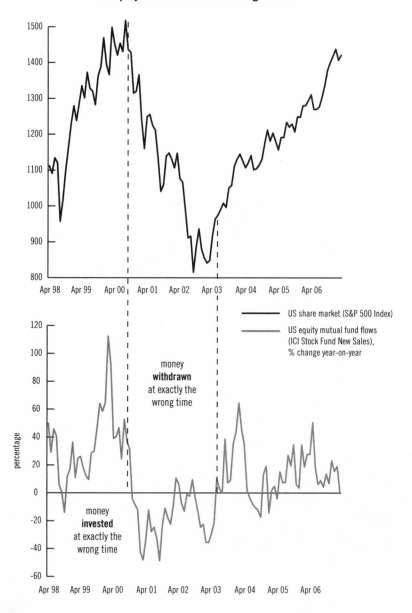

U.S. stock market performance compared with U.S. equity mutual fund flows during "bubble"

Source: Bloomberg, ICI, ipac

December 2000 and January 2001, by which time the market had already fallen almost 20 percent from its peak. The party was well and truly over.

According to figures from Morgan Stanley, much of the outflow from the mainstream market went straight to funds focusing on the overblown technology sector. This proved to be the worst place to hide, with the tech-heavy Nasdaq Composite Index crashing to end the year 2000 down almost 50 percent from its high point. By mid-2008 the Nasdaq was still trading at less than half its peak level achieved eight years earlier.

So why do investors keep making the same old mistakes? Why is it so hard to capture the Investment Prize?

REFLECTIONS: Do you feel more comfortable putting money into the markets when all the news is good or when all the news is bad? What is likely to be the better time to invest?

HOW OUR BRAINS ARE HARDWIRED

Our brains like things to be nice and simple. Take Newton's Law of Gravity. Once you know what it is, you understand that it never changes. You drop an apple and gravity does its job in an entirely predictable way. You don't need to know *how* it works, just that it does. It's a fixed system.

Complex systems are different. In these, it is almost impossible to work out the relationships among the different elements. It's hard to know what affects what.

The weather is a good example. After centuries of research, and with all our extraordinary technology, our ability to forecast the weather over anything but the shortest period is still embarrassingly poor. Yet meteorologists continue to improve their models, and it is possible that one day an accurate long-range weather prediction system will emerge.

The one thing meteorologists have going for them is that the components of weather—pressure gradients, wind speed, temperature, humidity, and so on—have fairly fixed relationships with one another. We know, for example, that a cold wind reduces temperature.

The stock market is a classic example of the hardest system of all to interpret, a complex adaptive system. This involves rules changing constantly as market participants learn from experience. The weather doesn't do that. Just as microbes learn from interactions with drugs and are able to change their form, participants in the stock market also modify their behavior. This is why there's no rule book for the stock market that works all the time. A vast number of factors, both external and internal to a company, affect the value of each stock. But the impact of particular factors is difficult to assess.

The problem for average investors is that they treat the stock market as a simple system, where the rules are fixed: do this, and that results. They spend their time looking for the rule book rather than focusing on strategies that will help them succeed.

By investing in a quality, diversified portfolio of shares, available from any number of competent fund managers, it's actually quite easy to capture the Investment Prize. Yet the distractions for investors are becoming greater, as volatility within individual stocks increases.

Strategic Economic Decisions Inc., (SED) founded by Horace "Woody" Brock, has consistently produced some of the most insightful research on the implications of people's behavior for the economy and investment markets. (More information is available at their website: www.sedinc.com.) SED argues that there's a common catalyst behind the increasing propensity of markets and stocks to overshoot and undershoot "fair value." This catalyst is changed investor behavior, primarily the result of the impact of technology.

The company cites the following reasons for the increased risk in markets:

Investor response is more concentrated. You can access information on any stock or share 24 hours a day. The use of new technologies also means that the timing edge which professional investors used to have over individuals has evaporated. Whereas stocks that disappointed the market in the past saw their share prices decline over days or weeks, stocks are now bought and sold on the same day, in response to the same news. Larger price reactions are the result. After declining gradually for a number of weeks, shares in the investment bank Bear Stearns opened on Friday, March 14, 2008, at $54.24. By the following Monday the shares were trading at just over $3.

Greater focus on short-term results. In an age of packaged investment products, a glut of data available on the performance of fund managers has increased the focus of consumers and fund managers on short-term performance.

Fund managers compete fiercely for clients, many of whom will not tolerate periods of low performance even if there are good reasons. For example, clients abandoned value-style share managers during the technology-stock bubble, when performance fell far short of that of growth-style managers. Yet the value-style managers owned better quality stocks at cheaper prices, as was shown when the market bubble burst and value-style stocks became the new flavor of the month during the early 2000s. The tide turned yet again toward growth-style managers in 2007.

Increased uncertainty about valuing stocks. Technology makes it harder to value stocks. Even for the best analyst, it can be far from clear which "pricing model" should be used to determine the value of an asset, for which there might be no precedent. An example is an Internet stock. What use, for example, is a price-earnings ratio for a stock with no predictable earnings?

Confusion can lead to trend-following behavior in individual stocks and sectors, causing both over- and underreactions to news. Stock prices move higher or lower than they otherwise might.

Infectious beliefs among investors. Uncertainty about how to value stocks also causes investors' beliefs to become influential. Often messages about what to believe come from a limited number of celebrity stock analysts and a handful of sources of information. From these the market sets expectations.

This was particularly so during the tech bubble, when glowing stock assessments from "A team" analysts like Abby Joseph Cohen of Goldman Sachs would often send a stock surging higher. Comments by the chairman of the Federal Reserve can also have profound and immediate effects on the American and global markets.

Greater use of borrowed money to invest. The greater use of borrowed money to invest, called "leverage," made possible by today's technologies, adds to the distractions. Margin lending, a form of investment in which the investor's own capital is topped up by a loan from a margin lender to increase the amount invested, has now hit the mainstream. Derivatives, including futures contracts, options to buy or sell investments in the future, and an endless array of even more complex financial products only add to the risk and volatility in markets. Many commentators, for example, blamed hedge funds, with their heavy usage of both leverage and derivatives, for worsening the downturn in world stock markets stemming from the subprime mortgage fiasco in mid-2007.

It is the combination of these factors, rather than any single one, that is most potent, SED argues.

It seems certain that periodic bouts of wealth destruction on a grand scale will continue, with adverse outcomes for investors in coming decades. However, individuals can avoid the worst of the herd mentality. The Investment Prize will be there for those with the patience to maintain sensible investment strategies in the face of bouts of speculative fever.

So forget those factors you cannot control, such as whether share or property markets will rise or fall this year or next. Build a well-diversified portfolio and focus on the single factor that will make the biggest difference to your success as an investor—your behavior.

Chapter 8

THE MADNESS OF MYOPIA

IF WE NOW KNOW THAT THE RETURN FROM SHARES has been higher than the return from bonds and cash, and that this is likely to continue, there is still one important question to ask: Why is it so much higher?

This has baffled researchers for years. Investors do, of course, demand compensation for the extra risk of investing in shares. But with a premium of 5–7 percent annually on average over the long term, the Investment Prize has been far richer than any theory suggests it should be.

Opinions in the research community vary widely on the so-called equity premium puzzle. But one persuasive view is that disciplined investors with a genuine long-term perspective on their share portfolios benefit from the mistakes made by others as markets rise and fall. Put another way, those investors who can't live with the emotional roller coaster of stock markets, and therefore invest too little in shares, create an opportunity for those with the patience and discipline to succeed in the market.

Let's now look briefly at the link between the price of an investment and the return on it. We will then examine in more detail the emotions unleashed when people lose money on their investments and how this drives their behavior.

WHAT IS A GOOD INVESTMENT RETURN?

An investment in a share is really very simple. It gives shareholders the right to be part of the future profits of a company and any growth in its asset price.

Of course, no one knows what those future profits will be, nor how they will translate into changes in the price of shares. A bewildering array of forces can affect the share price and profitability of the company. But ultimately, all investors come up with their best estimates of its future value and how much they should pay, often sourcing these estimates from stockbrokers. The return they end up with is simply the gap between what they pay today and what the value turns out to be in the future.

Suppose you buy a portfolio of shares that, one year later, is valued at $150,000. If you were overoptimistic and paid more than $150,000, you face a loss. Conversely, the less you paid, the bigger your profit.

What determines how much people pay? The answer is the same thing that determines most prices: supply and demand. The starting point that professional investors use to value shares is the return they can get from cash. This return comes with hardly any risk, so they "discount" the expected return from the asset by the cash rate. This means that the price they pay for the asset needs to be at least low enough to compensate for the risk-free alternative. They also apply a second discount for the risk of the asset itself. The greater the risk, the bigger the discount applied and the lower the price.

The less you pay, the more chance you have of getting a good return. The price of an asset reflects the level at which, collectively, investors expect to get a reasonable future return. Too high, and other investors sell the asset, driving the price down. Too low, and they buy more, pushing the price up.

The Profit Principle

The figure on the next page shows the return received, depending on the price paid today. Clearly, at any price above $150,000, the investors paid too much. They experienced a loss of 25 percent, for example, if they paid $200,000.

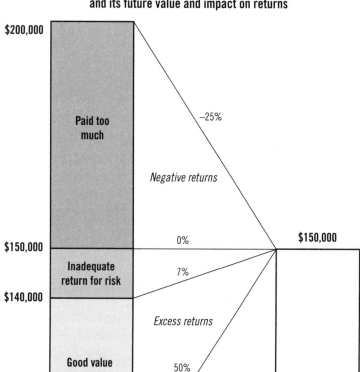

**The price paid today for a share portfolio,
and its future value and impact on returns**

Price paid today based
on estimate of future
value of portfolio

Future value of
share portfolio

At any price below $150,000, the investors started to make money. But it may be that, taking into account the return on cash as well as the risk of the portfolio, a return of less than 7 percent (that is, paying $140,000 or more) does not provide a decent reward for the risk taken.

On the other hand, if the investors were able to buy the portfolio for much less than this price, say $100,000, producing a return of 50 percent, then they would have enjoyed returns higher than were required to compensate for the risk.

If the premium from investing in a broadly diversified portfolio of shares has averaged between 5–7 percent annually over time, this is far higher than you might expect, given that over the long term the extra risk of shares compared with cash is not very great. The Investment Prize reflects the fact that people collectively invest too little in shares, causing today's price to be too low in relation to future value. To see why, it's important to understand how people react to the prospect of loss and the sense of regret, how they measure the returns on their portfolio, and how these factors lead to poor investment decisions.

THE PAIN OF LOSS IS STRONGER THAN THE PLEASURE OF GAIN

While investors are often accused of being risk averse, most are in fact not motivated by the desire to avoid risk. What they really want to avoid is actual financial loss—and most will pay good money to do so.

Dr. Kahneman and his colleague Amos Tversky took a close look at investor attitudes to gains and losses. Their research centered on the emotional impact that gains and losses of equal size could cause. They reached the startling conclusion that the pain of loss is about *twice as great* as the pleasure of an equivalent gain.

Kahneman and Tversky gave their research, published in 1979, the name "prospect theory." Their findings flew in the face of classical economics, which makes the assumption that all investors make "rational" decisions. For the first time, research measured how much people disliked losses and, by extension, how much they would pay to avoid a loss.

How Loss Averse Are You?

A quiz compiled by Kahneman with Mark Riepe for the *Journal of Portfolio Management* demonstrates how loss aversion affects decisions.

Question 1: Imagine that you are richer by $20,000 than you are today, and that you face a choice between two options.

A: Receive $5,000; or

B: A 50 percent chance to win $10,000 and a 50 percent chance to win nothing.

Question 2: Imagine that you are richer by $30,000 than you are today, and that you face a choice between two options.

A: Lose $5,000; or

B: A 50 percent chance to lose $10,000 and a 50 percent chance to lose nothing.

Which options would you choose? If you're like most people, say the authors, "You paid little attention to the initial statement before the options; you feel the two problems are quite different; and you chose the sure thing (Option A) in Question 1 and the gamble (Option B) in Question 2."

In fact, in terms of total expected wealth, the problems are identical. The choice in both cases is between being $25,000 richer, or taking a bet that results in being either $20,000 or $30,000 richer.

A rational decision maker, seeking only to maximize the financial outcome, would take either the sure thing in both questions or the gamble in both, rather than switching between options, depending on how the question was framed.

Most people choose Option A in Question 1 because they like the certainty of a $5,000 gain and don't want to risk a loss. Most people choose Option B in Question 2 because they dislike the certainty of a definite $5,000 loss so much that they will risk an even bigger loss in an attempt to avoid any loss at all.

SWAPPING A PEN FOR A LOTTERY TICKET: REGRET   In a further twist, research suggests that investors hate the way a loss makes them feel even more than they fear the loss itself. It seems that the emotional impact of a loss, in particular the sense of regret, may have an equal or greater effect than the financial loss itself. Loss hurts the wallet but regret strikes the heart.

Psychological research suggests that people are far more willing to swap tangible items such as pens than they are to exchange lottery tickets of the same face value. They don't want to risk the profound sense of regret that would follow giving away a winning lottery ticket.

Regret is a powerful emotion. It is hardwired into the brain by experience. If a certain activity has caused pain in the past, we are less likely to engage in it again. This is merely a natural survival mechanism. But it's unwise to let the prospect of regret affect your investment behavior.

Why Loss Aversion Is a Wealth Hazard

Kahneman and Tversky's observation on loss aversion helps explain why investors find it hard to take the risks that are necessary to achieve long-term goals, particularly in retirement planning.

Taking investment risks involves accepting the possibility both of making a loss and of experiencing regret. Risk-averse investors are seeking to avoid short-term regret, but such an ostrich response may well lead to even more profound regret later in life. The implication is that we must work against the brain's response mechanism that says it is more important to get through today than worry about the future. Risk-averse investors may avoid a temporary loss, but in so doing they also lose the probability of significant long-term gain.

WHY THE INVESTMENT PRIZE IS SO GENEROUS

Loss aversion provides part of the answer to the question posed at the start of the chapter. However, research has shown that investors would have to be loss averse to a ridiculous extent for this to explain the full 5–7 percent equity risk premium.

There has to be another reason why the Investment Prize is so large. In 1995, economists Benartzi and Thaler put forward a convincing explanation they called "myopic loss aversion."

It works like this. Suppose you have the choice of investing in either of two assets:

- A risky asset expected to return 7 percent annually on average, but subject to all the ups and downs of the market
- An asset that pays a guaranteed 1 percent return

How attractive you find the risky asset will depend on a range of factors, none more vital than your investment time horizon.

For an investment over a single year, an allocation to the risky asset would be considered a gamble. You could lose 20 percent or more of your investment in that time. Of course, you could also make a gain of a similar size.

Over a five-year time frame, however, the risky asset would start to look more attractive. This is because that length of time should generally allow for markets to recover from a fall. The chances of beating the 1 percent return are high.

Over a ten-year time frame, the "risky" asset would appear even more attractive.

The figure below shows the likely range of returns for international stock markets for periods from one to twenty-five years. Based on ipac securities'

Likely range of returns for international stock markets

modeling, returns are likely to fall into these ranges 95 percent of the time. For example, over a year, returns are likely to be as high as 37.9 percent or as low as -16.7 percent. Over a twenty-five-year period, however, the likely range of returns is much smaller; they are very likely to be positive and in the range of 1.9 percent to 12.7 percent, on average.

The graph below shows that returns from the U.S. stock market since 1901 have varied dramatically over one-year periods. However, returns over ten-year periods have been more stable and usually positive.

We can see from these examples that while the innate qualities of the risky asset have not changed, increasing the time horizon has reduced the risk. Over a thirty-year period, there may be little reason to invest in the "safe" asset at all. The expected premium from the risky investment would now be so large, and the risk so reduced by time, that the bulk of our money could be allocated to the risky investment with reasonable security.

Why the Reporting Period Is Critical

The investment time horizon, from the start of the investment period, is an important factor that influences investment decisions.

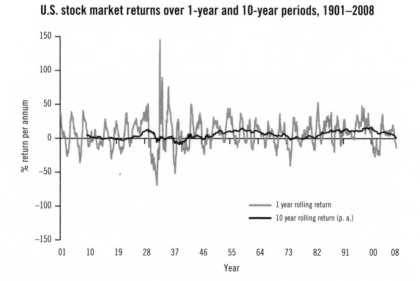

U.S. stock market returns over 1-year and 10-year periods, 1901–2008

Suppose that even if you have invested for thirty years, you receive a report every six to twelve months from the manager of the risky asset showing you its price. This level of reporting is a statutory obligation for managers of pension plans and mutual funds in most countries, to protect investors from unethical or incompetent operators.

Do these performance updates affect investors' decisions?

During periods when the asset performs well, there's no problem. But when account balances fall, it may be a different story. In fact, researchers find that investors who check their returns over short time periods are likely to be influenced more by their evaluation period, the frequency with which they check returns, than by their investment time horizon. If they don't like what they find, they will sell some, or all, of the risky asset, despite its long-term prospects. Such shortsightedness might also mean that they have bought less of the asset in the first place.

Investors will make decisions to minimize the likelihood of loss over six to twelve months, rather than focusing on ten, twenty, or thirty years. While the real time frame for investing may be thirty years, investors make decisions as though it is the period between fund reports. The shorter the evaluation period, the less likely an investor is to include a risky asset in a portfolio. Those investors who evaluate their portfolio returns less frequently are usually willing to take more risk. This will help them realize the full potential of investment markets and capture the Investment Prize.

Myopic loss aversion means that investors treat the long term as a series of short terms. Each decision is inadvertently framed with this perspective in mind. In his excellent book *Beyond Greed and Fear: Understanding Behavioral Finance and the Psychology of Investing*, leading behavioral finance researcher Hersch Shefrin writes that such investors "frame every gamble they face in isolation from all the others . . . as a one-shot deal, rather than as one more turn on the multi-road gamble of life."

The more frequently investors evaluate their returns, the more likely they are to make inappropriate short-term decisions. This is something frequently encountered by financial advisers when they conduct portfolio reviews with clients.

REFLECTIONS: How do you feel if you see a negative return
on an investment over a six-month period? What is the impact
on your decision making? What questions do you ask?

ANOTHER CAUTIONARY FABLE

The Hare and the Tortoise

To consider how this works in practice, consider the story of Quincy and
Caroline. The American research firm DALBAR has created a story around
this hypothetical couple to bring to life the behaviors that cause investors
to either capture or lose the Investment Prize.

Quincy and his wife Caroline inherited $20,000 in 1985. Quincy heard
that mutual funds were the best way to put money away, and he and Caroline decided that they would put their windfall into these. They decided
that they would split the money and each put $10,000 in their own account.
They both selected the same share fund and put their money in on the first
business day in January 1986.

In the twenty years since that time, Quincy stayed on top of the market,
checking on how his investment was doing every month. Caroline was
more concerned about raising their kids and would listen to Quincy talk
about how much he was making and, occasionally, how much he had lost.

A year after their initial investment, Quincy was very happy with his
decision. The investment was now worth $12,000 and so was Caroline's.

After two years, in October 1987, Quincy was worried about the news
of the market crash. When he checked on his investment balance, it had
fallen from $12,000 a year earlier to $9,600. He decided to limit any further loss and withdrew half, putting $4,800 in his checking account. He
wanted Caroline to do the same thing with her $9,600, but she talked it
over with a friend, a financial adviser, who assured her that the market
would eventually bounce back. She decided against doing anything.

By August of the following year, Caroline's account was back to $12,000.
Quincy still had $4,800 in his checking account that had not increased
when the market rose. At the end of 1988, Quincy regained his courage

and put the money back into his mutual fund. By this time Caroline's account was worth $15,000 and Quincy's was worth only $12,300.

In the intervening years Caroline simply let her nest egg grow while Quincy moved money in and out of the market. He would read the market reports and talk with friends to find out what they were doing. When he became worried about losing his money, he would withdraw some, and when his confidence was restored, he would invest it again.

By the end of 2005, Quincy had built his initial $10,000 investment up to $21,422. Caroline had not touched her investment so it had suffered during times of market declines and recovered when the market did. By the end of 2005 Caroline's account was worth ...

(a) $15,687

(b) $32,123

(c) $94,555

What is your guess?

The return from the S&P 500 during this period was 11.9 percent per annum, which is what Caroline captured, thanks to her buy-and-hold strategy. After twenty years, this meant that Caroline's portfolio was worth $94,555, or more than four times Quincy's portfolio of $21,422!

Quincy suffered from myopic loss aversion in a big way. This explains

- Why even investors with a very long time horizon, say from ten to thirty years, may feel uncomfortable holding a large allocation of shares in their portfolios.

- Why shares are often underrepresented in individual retirement portfolios with a significant time before pensions are drawn.

- Why a large number of major pension funds with theoretically unlimited time horizons maintain high allocations of cash and bonds.

Trustees and institutional fund managers may also be influenced by the business imperative to produce competitive returns over periods that are far shorter than the investment time horizons of fund members. They may be overly influenced by the frequency with which they report returns to investors in their funds, and want to avoid criticism.

WHY THE MYOPIA OF OTHERS
IS GREAT NEWS FOR YOU

Myopic loss aversion explains why the Investment Prize for investing in shares is so large. In their research, Thaler and Benartzi set out to find what combination of loss aversion and portfolio evaluation period would explain the magnitude of the Investment Prize.

They found that the actual size of the historical equity risk premium (taken by the researchers as 6.5 percent) was consistent with investors evaluating portfolios once a year. This makes intuitive sense since most investors receive annual statements.

If investors moved to a two-year evaluation period, the study found, the Investment Prize, or the future return of shares above the risk-free rate of return on cash, would fall from 6.5 to 4.65 percent. People would immediately invest more in shares, driving current prices higher and future returns lower. Some of the return "cake" would be "eaten" now instead of saved for later.

With an average twenty-year evaluation period, share investors would be willing to pay so much more for shares today that the Investment Prize of the future would fall to just 1.4 percent. The opportunity for genuine long-term investors is that individuals with a planning horizon of twenty years, less than the average time spent in retirement, have been rewarded by 5.1 percent extra annual return (the total 6.5 percent risk premium, less 1.4 percent attributable to loss aversion).

As long as investors keep reacting as they do to those annual fund statements, there is little chance this will change any time soon. The continuing myopic view of the majority is a pretty safe bet. You can take advantage of this.

To return a moment to Warren Buffett, one of the keys to his investment success has been his willingness to embrace volatility. He recognizes that those who have the mental resilience to weather rises and falls will win the Investment Prize. He says, "I have always preferred a bumpy 15 percent return to a smooth 12 percent return." We need to build the mental fortitude to follow suit.

Chapter 9

HOW TO BE PRUDENT AND TAKE THE LONG VIEW

WHY DO SHORT-TERM RETURNS FROM RISKY INVESTMENTS have such a profound impact on people's decisions? Why can't such returns be used to make good investment decisions? And how can you know if something has gone wrong in your portfolio—or indeed if something is going blissfully right—if recent returns don't tell you?

The most obvious reason why share portfolio returns measured over short periods have such an influence on investor behavior is volatility. As we saw in the last chapter, returns jump around a lot within short time frames, depending on the type of fund or fund manager.

Even for investors who accept that volatility is inevitable when taking on growth assets, this can be emotionally unsettling.

Imagine that you have never flown in a plane. On your first flight, you have been warned to expect turbulence and told that airplanes can withstand far more than they ever encounter. However, when the bumps begin, your mind starts racing. Is this normal? What's causing it? How do I know it will end? Is something wrong? Meanwhile, more experienced travelers may be calmly reclining, reading magazines, or watching an in-flight movie.

Investing in a share-based portfolio is like your first flight. You may know rationally that statistically the odds are heavily stacked in your favor. That doesn't necessarily stop you from being nervous. The most important behavioral attribute in your armory is to keep perspective during these periods.

WHY SHORT-TERM SHARE RETURNS OFFER SUCH A BUMPY RIDE

Share values jump around because they reflect background market "noise" rather than the continuing long-term trends that create wealth. The shorter the evaluation period, the more noise there is in price and performance.

In his book *Fooled by Randomness*, a study of the chance events and patterns that shape investment markets and so people's lives, Nassim Nicholas Taleb provides an example of a happily retired dentist who is an excellent investor.

Taleb's dentist expects to earn 15 percent annually in excess of Treasury bills, with 10 percent risk or volatility. This means that out of one hundred statistical samples, 68 would fall within a range of 5–25 percent (plus or minus 10 percent) around his 15 percent expected excess return.

The dentist also spends most of his days locked in his attic office, where he subscribes to a Web-based service that provides constant updates on the securities in his portfolio.

The probability that he will make money in *any one year* is 93 percent, a pretty fair bet. In other words, if he looks at a statement every year for the next twenty years, he should feel the pain of loss only once or twice.

His probability of making money over *any one quarter* in the next twenty years is 77 percent. So, if he receives quarterly statements, he feels the pain of loss about once each year. His probability of making money over *any given month* is 67 percent, and over *any given day* just 54 percent.

Assuming the dentist is glued to the screen every second of his day, the probability of making money in *any given second* is barely better than even, at 50.02 percent.

Now, it is impossible for the dentist to remain emotionally detached from the events unfolding on his screen. He feels every agonizing second. And since losses loom much larger in his eyes (as in everyone else's) than gains, he is likely to make decisions that, were he monitoring his portfolio once a year, he would never make.

Taleb takes his example one step further by analyzing the ratio of "noise" to "non-noise," or meaningful investment information in the price-feeds the dentist receives in his attic: "Over one year we observe roughly 0.7 parts 'noise' for every one part of performance. Over one month, we observe roughly 2.32 parts 'noise' for every one part of performance. Over one hour, 30 parts 'noise' for every one part performance, and over one second, 1,796 parts 'noise' for every one part performance."

This presents a huge problem when we attempt to assess the recent performance of our investments. While most investors expect reported returns from their fund managers to be accurate, to mirror the experience of others in the fund, to offer insight into the manager's skill, and even to provide a crystal ball for the future, if they do any of these things, it will be by accident rather than design.

Whatever the risk/return outcomes you expect from your own portfolio, it is clear from Taleb's dentist, and the actual experience of countless investors worldwide, that recent returns achieved by funds and fund managers mean a lot less than we might think. Usually, there's as much noise reflected in the number as there is true investment performance. Far from the latest return being the most important, the shorter and more recent the time period, the less meaningful it is.

WHY INVESTORS FOLLOW WINNERS AND END UP AS LOSERS

The simple explanation for why investors often end up losers when they follow winning stocks is that they apply rules of thumb in order to make sense of complex situations. One of the most common of these is to use the price of an asset as an indication of its quality—in other words, to view the most highly priced investment as the best.

To see why this is so, let's consider the simple example of buying a shirt at the local department store. Most people know the difference between a well-made shirt and one of inferior quality, so when quality shirts are on sale, it makes sense to buy more. That's why consumers break down doors in the post-Christmas sales.

Remarkably, in the stock market, exactly the opposite behavior takes place. Investors avoid those shares or funds where the price has fallen—those that are effectively on sale—and snap up those where the price (or performance in the case of a managed fund) has recently risen.

Why? Because, in contrast to evaluating a shirt, it is much harder to evaluate whether or not a company is of superior quality. This makes investors apply a simple mental shortcut: using price to evaluate quality. They tell themselves, if the price is high, it must be a good investment; if the price is low, it must be inferior. This leads to the obvious outcome: where investors buy the most highly priced investments, those are the ones with the least potential for future price rises.

Thus, investors actually buy more quality "shirts" when the price goes up than they do when they are on sale. If you did this when actually buying clothes, your family would think you were mad.

Let's take another example. Imagine you are an investor in two funds: one a share fund that has fallen 5 percent for the quarter, and one a bond fund that has gained 5 percent. Your portfolio statement arrives and the apparent "loss" on the share fund is causing you sleepless nights. Your partner has started to complain about your foul mood.

You respond by selling the share fund and directing your money toward the apparent safety of bonds. Three months later, the next statement arrives. This time it's a 9 percent return for shares and -1 percent return for bonds. You sell bonds, buy shares, and wait for the next statement.

While both markets have posted net gains over the combined period, you, the investor, have missed both by moving between assets at just the wrong time.

This classic investment trap is played out constantly, as managers and funds tend to deliver their best results after periods of low returns and their worst returns after boom times. By jumping onto the bandwagon of past winners, investors end up as losers. The shorter the period, the more useless are the funds' published returns, with the most recent return being the most useless of all. Just as a corporate balance sheet gives a one-off snapshot of a company's position at a specific time, a position that changes before the ink dries, so too does your fund's or manager's return reflect a one-off position that may also change overnight. Unlike a balance sheet, however, each performance measurement period has both a start and an end date, so the potential for distortion is exaggerated.

For each performance end date there are literally hundreds of start dates for individual investors, and for each start date (when money is first invested) there will be hundreds or thousands of end dates, many of them not yet reached. This is why few investors ever receive their funds' published returns over three-, six-, or twelve-month periods.

The difference that even a few days makes to what is in your fund's report is remarkable. Investors who bought the American S&P 500 on February 21, 2005, and sold their shares two years later on February 20, 2007, achieved a share price return of 13.7 percent, while those who bought and sold the same portfolio two weeks later achieved a return of just 7.5 percent.

Short-term performance data are no more than a statistical sampling at a moment in time: an investor's equivalent to musical chairs. But while this childhood game depends on luck alone, fund managers with a seat when the music stops will still be in the game due to skill, luck, or other factors.

THREE PATHWAYS TO THE SAME RESULT

The figure below shows just three examples of the many different pathways that individual funds may take over time. It is an example of the

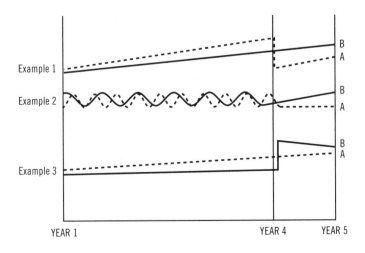

two-point performance comparisons that populate fund return columns in performance tables and investor reports. Most people, even qualified financial advisers, make investment decisions based on these tables. They can, however, be seriously misleading.

> **Example 1:** If you looked at a return comparison between Fund A and Fund B, assuming you bought at the start of Year 1 and sold at the end of Year 5, at the end of the full five-year period, Fund B would have produced the highest return. But for four of the five years, Fund A actually did better than Fund B. Fund performance tables won't reveal this important information.

> **Example 2:** Fund B produced the highest return over the full five-year period. But for four of the five years, either Fund A or Fund B could have delivered better performance, depending on the exact date of measurement. Fund B had one good year (for unknown reasons that may not be repeated), and its five-year performance history is elevated to a higher category. Performance tables won't reveal that, either.

> **Example 3:** Fund B produces the highest return over the full five-year period. But for four of the five years, Fund A produced the best result.

Fund Performance: Skill or Luck?

Do reported performance numbers for professionally managed funds reflect skill or luck? Statisticians are still arguing about whether it takes fifty, sixty, or seventy years to find out, although all agree it takes a long time. In any large sample of managers or funds, a significant number will have outperformed by sheer chance.

During World War II, a South African prisoner of war with a penchant for probability theory is reputed to have tossed a coin 10,000 times to see if the chances of heads or tails were indeed 50/50. He found they were. He recorded each toss and was amazed to see that the longest sequence was fifty-six heads in a row. Yet this was pure chance. It's a simple game and we know the odds.

Now apply this lesson to the complex world of portfolio management, where the true odds are far from obvious. Fund managers get lucky—the investment equivalent of achieving fifty-six heads in a row—all the time. Funds produce the right results for the wrong reasons, or the wrong results for the right reasons, far more often than most investors realize.

The truth is that fund performance numbers, even over quite long periods, may reflect little more than luck. This doesn't mean you should ignore past performance altogether. Just recognize that it is only one indicator of possible future results—and not a very reliable one.

REFLECTIONS: To what extent does past fund performance influence your judgment about which investments to buy? Have you ever bought an investment with a poor recent track record? What was the outcome?

HOW WE CAN RESPOND

Understanding myopic loss aversion and the limitations of reported returns and fund league tables published in newspapers and magazines is only the beginning. Taking action to keep perspective, to ensure that we aren't blinded by myopia, and capturing the Investment Prize that results from the shortsightedness of others are more difficult.

Here are some practical strategies to help you succeed.

Have a plan that takes into account your real time horizon for investing, not your evaluation period. For most investors, a comprehensive plan means one developed with a qualified financial adviser and that plans for life goals and is supported by a sound investment strategy. However, there is evidence that a plan of any sort, even one not necessarily written down or developed with a qualified adviser, can provide better results than no plan at all.

When it comes to investing money, there are various ways to allocate funds. For example, an adviser may suggest a "pools," or "time horizons," approach, where your money is allocated to different pools, each with a different time period, depending on your cash needs at various times.

With this approach, spending needs for (say) the next two years may be quarantined in a secure cash fund or a low-volatility portfolio. If you are planning for retirement and have no immediate spending needs because you are still earning, this would most likely see most of your money allocated to growth-oriented funds with a significant share allocation.

Check your fund returns regularly, but keep perspective. While the last two chapters showed that frequent monitoring of fund returns can lead to overly conservative portfolios and poor investment decisions, it is unrealistic and unwise to "set and forget" a portfolio for the long term. Remember, what matters is not so much the fact that investors check the numbers on their statements each quarter, as *how they respond to them.*

In many jurisdictions, quarterly or semiannual reports to investors are now required. It is certainly sensible to check these to see how your fund and fund manager are performing, and to ensure they are investing your money in the agreed way.

However, it is important to look behind the numbers in a report to the real drivers of performance. That involves understanding the investment strategy, a framework for which is explained in chapter 11.

Investment return is not the same as investment performance; it is essential to look at returns in context. As we saw in the earlier examples involving Fund A and Fund B, any reasonable evaluation of performance should take into account not just actual investment returns but also an assessment of how these were generated.

Such assessment includes the risks involved; special prevailing circumstances; whether or not such returns can be repeated; whether luck has played a significant role—and so on. This is not easy, but it is well worth the effort.

Most fund managers provide the qualitative context for their performance, enabling us to assess the true drivers of returns, although some may need prompting to provide the next layer of data, such as major fund holdings. Research services that study professionally managed funds can also assist with this task.

Distinguish between "good" and "bad" outperformance and underperformance. Sometimes a fund manager has performed well, but their returns are low, or they have managed their funds poorly but returns are high. Why?

It depends on the circumstances. The important point is that outperformance or underperformance compared with a market index or with other fund managers can be for the right or wrong reasons. If a fund has a value-oriented investment style, and looks predominantly for companies trading at cheap prices, such a fund would not be expected to perform well during periods when conditions favor the fastest-growing companies.

For example, during the technology-stock bubble in the late 1990s, when value managers such as the well-known American-based Sanford Bernstein (now AllianceBernstein) significantly underperformed in that stock market, there were good reasons for this. Fast-growing companies were the darlings of the stock market, while Sanford Bernstein had promised investors it would fish in other ponds with their money. It kept that promise, and in time investors were well rewarded.

It would have been far more worrisome to own a value fund that delivered spectacular returns during the technology-stock bubble than one that struggled. This may well have been a sign that the manager had abandoned its long-term value-focused strategy and had instead chased market momentum. This would be a sign of "bad" outperformance that would eventually have adverse repercussions.

Past returns are a poor guide to the future. Studies have consistently shown that past returns, even where a long track record exists, are typically a poor guide to future ones. In fact, most studies show that investors would be better off with the fund that delivered the lowest return in the past, rather than the highest. This is another good reason to look behind the numbers to see what's really driving returns.

Use a good financial adviser. Some people can plan their finances well, without professional help. However, good advice can make the whole process easier and relieve much of the responsibility for the construction and monitoring of a portfolio. Financial advisers may take on the more technical aspects themselves, or outsource these to specialists while they focus on clients' needs and goals by providing strategy-based advice.

Behavioral finance researchers Kenneth Fisher and Meir Statman describe the role of a good financial adviser as akin to that of an optometrist: he or she "correct(s) the vision of investors and lead(s) them to prudent decisions." In chapter 12 we suggest what to look for in such an adviser.

Armed with the strategies outlined in this chapter, you will be well placed to counter the effects of myopic loss aversion and the distractions of market noise.

Chapter 10

THE PUZZLING PROPERTIES
OF PROPERTY

FOR MOST PEOPLE, BUYING A HOUSE TO LIVE IN has always provided the strongest inducement to save money. The discipline of monthly mortgage repayments is an extremely strong motivator, but it is often also a source of stress.

In Maslow's hierarchy of needs, the need for safety, including shelter and security, ranks behind only such basic physiological needs as breathing, eating, and drinking. It's no wonder that owning residential property is popular.

The stock market has produced higher investment returns than residential property over the long term. This means in theory that those who rent a property and invest their money in the stock market should be wealthier than those who concentrate on paying off their homes.

However, the reality is that simply meeting regular mortgage payments and gradually taking ownership of a tangible asset means that homeowners usually do better financially than those who rent. But beware: a strong preference for property can lead to overinvestment. This can be dangerous for your overall wealth.

If stock market investors tend to be shortsighted and underinvest, property investors go to the opposite extreme. Research conducted by *The Economist* magazine found that between 1980 and 2003, a period in which both shares and property experienced boom-bust cycles more than once, shares significantly outperformed residential property in all the major economies. Investing in residential property other than your family home is likely to result in higher risk and lower returns than investing in quality shares.

This trend has held true over long periods of time. Using data from the United States from 1890–2004, the economist Robert Shiller calculated that inflation-adjusted home prices in the United States increased by just 0.4 percent annually. Shiller conducted similar analysis in Amsterdam, a city in which space has always been at a premium. He looked at it over a 350-year period, this time focusing on a single representative street. The level of investment returns was remarkably similar.

What drives investor behavior when it comes to buying residential property? And why do investors behave so differently with property and shares?

BUSINESS SUCCESS DRIVES PROPERTY PRICES

An economy in which business is performing well is likely to be one in which the property market is also growing strongly. One of the main reasons shares outperform property over long periods is that demand for property, in a market-based economy, is derived from the success of business. Thriving businesses create demand for both commercial property and residential property, both through their own expansion needs and via the attractive salaries they pay their staffs, who often then use the money to upgrade their properties. In tough times, businesses scale back their operations and lay off staff, thrusting this cycle into reverse. Excess supply in the commercial property market is an inevitable result of these downturns, causing prices in this sector to fall.

This occurred in technology parks around the world just after the turn of the century. However, residential property prices may also come under pressure during weak periods for business because of rising unemployment and slow or no growth in real wages, and associated lack of consumer confidence.

Of course, the business cycle and the property market do not work in perfect lockstep. There are periods of economic stagnation in which the property market enjoys a catch-up boom, and periods of recovery in which it goes through a down cycle.

Demographic and supply-and-demand issues also come into play. These vary dramatically from one market to the next. But over the long haul, the success of business and the economy drives property prices, not the other way around.

This derived demand for property is not, however, enough to explain the size of the gap in historical performance between shares and property that, depending on the market, has averaged around 3–5 percent annually. There must be another reason.

In fact, there are two other reasons: on average, the risks of investing in property are understated, and returns from investing in property are overstated.

As a result, investors pour too much money into residential property, forcing prices higher than they would be if they accounted fully for the potential risks and returns investors are likely to experience. As we saw with the stock market, this means less "future return" is left for long-term property investors.

CLASSIC TRAP: "YOU CAN'T GO WRONG WITH PROPERTY"

When stock markets fell early in 2000, real estate agents in major developed economies, particularly specific regions in the United States, the Netherlands, and Australia, were enjoying an unprecedented boom in business.

Share investors were going through the worst bear market in seventy years. For some, particularly among those who became shareholders for the first time in the 1980s and '90s, through holdings in superannuation or pension plans or the privatization of former government-owned businesses, there was an exodus to residential property. Shares were seen as simply too risky.

The fall in stock markets and rising residential property prices in many areas revived the well-worn but misleading advice that "you can't go wrong with property."

Forgotten after every bust and recycled with every boom, this reemerged to reflect perceptions that property is almost a risk-free investment. In turn, it led even sophisticated financial institutions to overinvest in property-based investments and to borrow too much against these investments, leading—in some cases—to their ruin.

Like the stock market, the property market moves in cycles, from boom to bust and back again. And just like the stock market, property cycles are unpredictable. As with shares, the price of property reflects future income-earning potential, discounted for the cash rate and additional risks. It simply goes against recorded history to think property prices can't fall.

An even more severe downturn was under way in the United States, where the residential property market peaked in December 2005 before entering its most painful and widespread fall in decades. By mid-2008 the market had fallen by more than 15 percent by some measures, with prices in some of the worst-hit metropolitan areas in California slumping more than 20 percent. Take inflation into account and the real loss was even worse. The mortgage delinquency rate in some areas of California, measured by the value of mortgages in arrears by thirty days or more, approached 10 percent.

What surprised many about the downturn was how geographically widespread the pain was distributed for such a large and diverse economy. Of the 200 metropolitan areas tracked by the *Wall Street Journal*, 113 had experienced price falls since the market's peak by mid-2008, and overall price falls were at a level not seen since the Depression of the 1930s.

There are five myths about property investment that resurface in every boom.

1. Property values are not as volatile as share prices.
2. Property prices never fall.
3. Property prices might fall occasionally, but never as far as share prices.
4. Property prices rise with the cost of living, so investment in property always keeps you ahead of inflation.
5. The only way to lose money on property is to buy into a declining population center, or a house on the main road.

Most of these myths stem from the belief that investing in property is a low-risk, low-volatility investment. As a general rule, this is incorrect.

While the measured *volatility* of property is indeed low, this is because the measurement systems are flawed. Property can in fact be one of the riskiest, most volatile investments. Many fortunes have been lost because investors did not comprehend the precipitous pace at which property markets can tumble. Property markets can fall for at least as long as stock markets, and just as far.

In Britain, the residential property market kept pace with the stock market for much of the second half of the twentieth century. Then in the 1990s, when shares boomed, residential property entered a five-year slump. Residential property prices fell due to a deep recession combined with falling inflation. More than 1 million buyers found themselves with negative equity in their homes. They were unable even to sell because their mortgages were larger than the value of their homes.

For those able to survive this difficult period, however, the second half of the 1990s brought a surging recovery, with strong price rises in Glasgow, Edinburgh, Manchester, and Birmingham, as incomes in these areas also spiraled upward. However, by late 2007 and into 2008, prices were again falling in some areas.

For Japanese investors during the past two decades, the property market has been as disastrous as the stock market. Hundreds of thousands of families have been similarly caught in a negative-equity trap, with average prices falling by more than 30 percent between 1997 and 2008.

Many people in other countries believe such calamities could never happen to them. Local conditions are in their favor, they believe. But in fact, virtually all property markets the world over experience downturns from time to time.

REFLECTIONS: What is your attitude to property investing and where does this attitude come from? Could your parents, friends, or others have had an influence? On balance, has this influence been good or bad for you?

WHY PROPERTY RISKS ARE UNDERSTATED

There are five main reasons why the risks associated with residential property investment are not well appreciated.

Property seems easy to understand, so investors have a perception of control. Property seems much easier to comprehend than shares or bonds. One of the reasons is that, unlike shares or bonds, it's a very concrete asset. You can drive past it, walk through it, renovate it, or give your friends a tour.

As real estate agents well understand, this gives property the power to elicit an emotional response, unlike most other investments. It is why auctions are often held on site. Experiencing the pull of an attractive property can encourage prospective buyers to use their hearts, not their heads.

While owning shares means becoming part owner of companies that usually hold physical assets, such as retail stores or factories, share certificates or electronic scrip are intangible and have no emotional content. You can't drive past your shares. You can't renovate them when something goes wrong.

Unless shareholders or fund investors take the time to visit the premises of the company, understand its strategy, and so on, owning shares or bonds lacks the sense of substance and permanence that attracts people to property.

Everyone believes they are property experts. Since so many people are homeowners, this is often seen as translating into general knowledge of the whole property market. This leads, in turn, to overconfidence, introducing risks.

Researchers have shown that people are generally overconfident of their abilities in areas they think they know well. Familiarity with the housing market for investors who have enjoyed a recent positive experience can lead to reduced perception of risks. Overconfidence is a feeling we will consider in more detail in the next chapter.

Property prices are artificially smoothed. The misconception that residential property is always safe and secure is compounded by the artificial smoothing of returns that results from the ad hoc way in which property is valued. Compared with the continuous disclosure and volumes of information and analysis available about publicly listed companies, the property market operates in a "London fog."

Imagine that you operate a business with a partner who is reasonably even-tempered most of the time, but who can explode in anger. These outbursts may last for an hour or two before your partner returns to his normal balanced state.

But this anger is beginning to affect your business together. As a condition of remaining in partnership, you arrange for him to undertake assessment by a clinical psychologist. If the psychologist were to visit once a week or once a month, she might never see your partner during one of the outbursts. She would have to take your word for it. If your partner refused to cooperate with the therapist, this might lead to the conclusion that there was nothing wrong. You might even be blamed for causing the whole situation.

However, if the psychologist were to wire up your partner electronically, to detect miniscule changes in temperament throughout the day, his true volatility would be detected and the assessment would be much more accurate.

In the same way, listed companies are "wired up" to stock exchanges that provide continuous evaluation and pricing. Prices of residential properties, as distinct from property trusts or real estate investment trusts listed on the stock market, are only infrequently evaluated. Volatile periods go undetected and are ignored in assessing risk.

Assessment of residential property is infrequent and informal. While your financial adviser or fund manager will provide regular assessments of the performance of your shares, funds, or listed real estate vehicles, correct to the decimal place, you will never receive reports on your residential property's performance, its rental income, and capital gain. Property investors never see red ink on a statement unless it is on the day of sale. And most property investors never formally evaluate the performance of their investments at all.

This is the opposite of the short evaluation periods symptomatic of myopic loss aversion in share investors. Property evaluation periods are generally very long or nonexistent. This makes property look relatively less risky than shares. It's not.

Property valuation systems are unreliable. The valuation systems that do exist for property are also far from foolproof. Typically, property value assessors compare those properties held in a portfolio with similar ones, assess sale prices and rentals in the same market segment, and produce a formal appraisal. This increases the chances of investors acting on misinformation.

The price of shares is based on the sale of identical units, with identical rights to dividends and earnings, so that all units are truly equal. But each property is unique. This means that property valuations are based on imperfect information, leaving them open to subjective judgment. They are also generally out of date even before they are produced because they are linked to transactions made in the past. The market may already have moved.

Overall, the valuation system is far better at providing an indication of what a property *should be worth* than what a property *is worth*. In the residential property market, the only true valuation occurs when a sale is finalized.

Commercial properties are usually valued at least annually or biannually so they can be revalued in the owner's books, providing much greater insight into volatility in prices and risk. And real estate investment trusts, just like publicly listed shares, are valued every minute of the day.

From the viewpoint of a rational investor, the factors outlined all make property investment seem a risky proposition, certainly riskier than conventional wisdom would allow. How safe is an investment whose value is difficult to determine?

REFLECTIONS: Do you believe you are better at valuing property or valuing shares? Why do you hold this belief? Does your experience suggest you are right or wrong?

WHY PROPERTY RETURNS ARE OVERSTATED

Just as the risks involved in property ownership are understated, returns achieved from property are overstated. This has the effect of further narrowing the risk/return trade-off for the asset.

Indexes that measure property market performance generally capture only the increase in sale price of existing dwellings. They usually fail to take into account major improvements in a nation's housing stock, whether achieved through new development or renovation of existing dwellings.

In the past few decades, the inner areas of major cities in most developed countries have been transformed from slums to lively, safe, and fashionable places to live.

Luxury apartment and townhouse complexes have sprung up in response to changing demographics: aging populations requiring smaller low-maintenance housing and baby boomers seeking the good life.

With the outsourcing of manufacturing to developing economies, just-in-time inventory management systems, and Internet-based shopping, warehouses lining waterways such as the Thames in London are now enjoying a second more sedate life as city pads for the wealthy. A similar revival has taken place in London's East End, with countless industrial sites turned into fashionable apartments, even attracting celebrities.

Similarly, brownstone terraces in New York's Harlem district, which once made headlines only for crime and urban decay, have undergone restoration at huge cost. Former President Bill Clinton famously established his offices in Harlem, lending further cachet to the area. In fact, so successful has the transformation of Harlem been that there are now fears that the character of the area will be destroyed as the longstanding families are forced out by the rising costs of living, which include exorbitant rents.

On the other side of the country, property in the famous Venice Beach area of Los Angeles used to be relatively cheap in the 1960s, and it certainly was not fashionable. But in recent decades the tide has turned as celebrities have moved in, including movie star Julia Roberts, who consolidated several blocks and built a substantial mansion there.

This trend has had a distorting effect on the way property prices are measured, including the reported size of capital gains. Returns from property are overstated for the same reason that risks are understated: flaws in measurement.

REFLECTIONS: Consider your experience with residential property, either an investment property or your family home. Calculate the difference between what you paid for the property and a conservative estimate of what it's worth today—your gross capital gain. Next, write down all your expenses in purchasing, maintaining, and renovating the property—from stamp duty and agents' fees, through general maintenance costs like roof repairs, and major renovations. Deduct this amount from the gross capital gain. How much is left? What return would this represent per annum since you bought the property?

NO ELECTRONIC SCOREBOARD FOR PROPERTY

Equity investors can effectively "buy the stock market" and participate in its long-term performance because of the ready availability of accumulation indexes that are net of costs incurred in achieving gains. For example, General Electric's valuation is based on the market's view of its expected earnings at any time, taking into account the costs incurred in achieving these.

Investors can't "buy" the return of the residential property market like this, because the sales measures available are gross of costs such as construction outlays. In other words, these measures track changes in asset values without making allowance for the very costs that make those values higher. Equity market indexes adjust constantly to reflect investors' perceptions of changes in the quality and value of companies represented in the index, while sales data for residential property do not.

In practical terms, investing in residential property has its own risks, which makes it more akin to investing in a single stock. While these risks can be mitigated through research into location, quality of property, and so on, opportunities for broad diversification and protection of a residential property investment portfolio are more restricted.

There have, of course, been genuine and sustainable rises in property prices in many markets, and there is every reason to believe that, notwithstanding the occasional price bubble, this will continue over the long term. Equally, however, there is every reason to believe that shares will continue to outperform property by a significant margin.

THE BOTTOM LINE

Just as myopic loss aversion in the stock market causes investors to hold overly conservative share allocations, excessive prudence and ignorance about risk in the property market causes many investors there to hold overly aggressive positions.

Risks in the stock market are obvious and exaggerated, while risks in property are less obvious and understated. But they are there, nonetheless. The result is systematic overinvestment in property that is at its worst in the residential sector.

An isolated period of overinvestment can deliver bumper returns, as the technology-stock bubble showed share investors. But returns that have been consumed today cannot be consumed again tomorrow. The effect is that property prices, bid to inflated levels and given their true risk/return characteristics, leave less room for future growth in prices relative to shares. As a result, shares are likely to continue to outperform residential property investments over the long term by a significant margin.

Applying the same principles as we did in our earlier discussion of myopic loss aversion to the residential property market, and assuming that prices for individual residential properties are just as volatile as the stock market, the theoretical outperformance of shares over property should similarly be 5.1 percent annually. In reality, over long periods it hasn't been too far from this.

Various other factors also suggest that there has been systematic overinvestment in residential property at the expense of shares. These include

- Tax systems in many countries that provide tax breaks for investing in residential property, particularly your own home, relative to other assets;
- The greater ease and lower cost of raising finance secured against property, in contrast with shares;
- The solid nature of property, which together with its perceived lower volatility, creates a greater sense of confidence in its safety.

SURF CASTING OR SURFING?

In sporting terms, property investors have much in common with surf casters while share investors can be compared with surfers.

Surf casting, while seemingly a benign and pleasant pastime, in fact ranks as one of the most dangerous recreational activities. In coastal areas, more people (adjusted for participation) die in surf casting accidents than from diving out of planes, hang gliding, surfing, motor racing, or almost any other seemingly more dangerous sport.

The reason why surf casting is dangerous is the same reason why it appears to be safe: the risks are invisible. The ocean is generally calm, but a rogue wave can sweep in over a rock platform with catastrophic results, even on a relatively calm day.

Surfing large waves, on the other hand, appears to be a dangerous sport, but it is actually fairly safe. Its risks are obvious and precautions can be taken. Someone who can't swim, for example, probably will not attempt to surf in the ocean but probably *will* attempt to go surf casting.

Similarly, stock markets offer visible risks. They are likely to continue to offer the Investment Prize above the risk-free rate of return and, generally, over the long term, more than the average return from quality property.

The one main advantage of investing in residential property is that individual investors with time on their hands have a greater ability to add value to their investments. They can conduct their own detailed market research on one of the many online services now available, or commit time and energy to a quality renovation that adds significant value to the property.

For many people, buying a family home is their one truly effective means of saving. But for the amateur investor who does not wish to become a property expert, investing in residential property is likely to be more expensive, more time-consuming, and riskier than investing in a well-run diversified share portfolio. And it will probably yield a lower return too.

Chapter 11

CONFRONTING THE ENEMY WITHIN

FOR MOST INVESTORS, THE ENEMY LURKS INSIDE. Whether investing in shares, property, or plain old cash deposits, we often lose perspective and make irrational decisions.

Yet there are simple, effective strategies we can use to overcome these hardwired instincts. In this chapter we explore the common mental mistakes made by investors, and how to avoid becoming a victim of the enemy within.

JUDGING A BOOK BY ITS COVER

Making judgments based on stereotypes, known as *representativeness*, is one of the most common mental mistakes. Every time we meet a new acquaintance, we know within seconds, certainly minutes, whether or not we are going to like this person. Occasionally, we really click with someone, experiencing instant rapport.

This ability to interpret a situation instantly is a survival mechanism that evolved to help us avoid threatening situations. However, relying on stereotypes to make financial decisions, rather than assessing facts, means that we may overreact to new information.

Researchers at the Federal Reserve Bank in New York have found that investors believe that shares in the best companies will perform the best. The strong performance and quality of a company is seen as representative of strong future share price performance. However, a high-quality company can produce dismal returns if its share price starts too high, while shares in an inferior company may do well over long periods if they are very cheap to begin with.

Similarly, the American academic and behavioral finance researcher Russell J. Fuller, in *Modern Investments and Security Analysis,* has observed that prices of companies that have recently announced big falls in profits often become much cheaper than is justified.

The reason is that many investors overreact, selling their shares and pushing prices down too far. This creates an excellent opportunity for those who are able to focus on longer-term expectations and buy, or hold, the stock at the right price.

SHORTCUTS THAT LEAD DOWN BLIND ALLEYS

"Everything should be made as simple as possible, but not simpler," observed Albert Einstein, one of history's greatest minds. Every minute of the day we use mental shortcuts or rules of thumb, called heuristics, to simplify decisions.

In a typical day we make countless choices: what to wear, how to get to work, whether or not to stop for coffee on the way—and, if so, whether to have a skinny flat white or a weak decaf latte with two sugars. Most choices and decisions involve little, if any, recognizable thought.

In *Influence: The Psychology of Persuasion,* Robert Cialdini argues that we need shortcuts to cope with daily life. "We must very often use our stereotypes, our rules of thumb, to classify things according to a few key features and then to respond mindlessly when one or another of these trigger-features is present."

But rules of thumb don't work in all situations.

Anyone who has seen the movie *Crocodile Dundee* will relate to the experience of Mick Dundee from outback Australia, played by actor Paul

Hogan, as he attempts to come to grips with life in New York City. Mick sleeps on the floor in his hotel room because he is used to roughing it at home, happily says "G'day" to everyone he passes on a teeming rush hour sidewalk, and, in the best-known scene, pulls out an enormous hunting knife when accosted by a street gang. These behaviors are critical for Mick's survival at home, but when he is transported to the Big Apple, they become unusual, even dangerous.

Similarly, investors make a huge mental mistake when they to apply rules of thumb in inappropriate circumstances. Here's a simple example that Dr. Fuller uses. Which of the two vertical line segments appears to be longer in the figure?

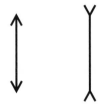

The line on the right appears longer, but in fact the two lines are the same length. The line appears longer, says Fuller, because the human brain is hardwired to interpret three-dimensional vision. In this case, the brain applies the same rule to lines drawn on a two-dimensional surface. The arrowheads trick the brain into thinking it is looking at a 3D object.

Look at the lines again: which looks longer now? Still the line on the right? That's not surprising. Even when we know a particular rule of thumb could lead us to a poor result, it is often still difficult to ignore the rule. However, we do so at our peril.

RULES OF THUMB AND PAST PERFORMANCE

The tendency to believe that past investment performance is a guide to future performance is a classic decision-making shortcut that leads to disaster.

What makes it so hard to resist this shortcut is that there are many other circumstances in which the general rule of thumb—that past performance is a guide to the future—works quite well.

Universities accept students with the highest grade-point averages. Buyers of secondhand cars choose those with the best track record. So do employers when vetting job candidates, and airline passengers when choosing between carriers.

Studies of cash flows into and out of mutual funds show that the average investor puts money into recent strong performers—and that this leads to poor results.

How many times has an acquaintance or even an adviser recommended a stock, fund, or asset class that has delivered poor performance in the past year?

If you're like most people, the answer is never. Now consider how many times you hear suggestions like these from people who have enjoyed short-term investment success: "My OHW shares have done well, you should get some!" Or "My BFM fund has gone through the roof. You'd be mad not to put some money in there." You won't hear a word more when OHW shares turn out to be a One Hit Wonder and BFM a Big Fat Mistake.

As we discussed in chapter 9, when a high-quality $99 shirt is discounted to $79, shoppers regard it as a bargain. However, when a good high-quality share or share fund falls in price and goes "on sale" in the market, investors avoid it. If the fund's price increases, however, making it the strongest performer in its category (that is, the fund's underlying assets become more expensive), it is widely regarded as an excellent investment and money floods in.

This makes no sense. Remember that when you buy investments that have recently made strong price gains, you are probably buying *expensive* assets.

REFLECTIONS: Have you ever made an investment based purely on the high returns it delivered in the past? What was the result? If successful, do you think this was the result of luck or skill?

You should not completely ignore performance when assessing investments. Just remember that performance history is one of many factors. A long track record of consistent performance is usually a good sign. But what if the team responsible for the strong past performance of a mutual fund left the company last month? What if the market conditions underpinning a dream run have changed? What if past performance was due to major holdings in one or two stocks that had done well? There are a thousand other "what ifs . . . ?"

Studies have shown that in many cases investors with a short-to-medium time horizon would be better off selecting funds from among the worst recent performers than from among the best.

"I Saw It with My Own Eyes"

Also destructive is the tendency to overemphasize major events, particularly those that occurred recently, a phenomenon known as *saliency*.

The shocking but perversely compelling images of planes crashing into the twin towers of the World Trade Center have been planted deep in our psyches. Live coverage of such overwhelming events sends the message "You are not safe." Many people then hugely overestimate the statistical probability of being killed or of suffering loss as a result of terrorist activities. This is part of the reason why the global aviation industry entered a steep decline following the attacks, and why September 11, 2001, will resonate with air travelers for years to come.

This is a natural human reaction, and a degree of fear of terrorism is justified. We do know, however, that two of the biggest steps people in Western societies can take to increase their safety are to wear seatbelts when driving and to stop smoking. Yet these are often regarded as far less risky than the possibility of being killed in an airplane crash, despite the minute statistical probability that this will occur.

Investors can be driven to distraction by placing too much weight on new and seemingly important information, while more powerful long-term trends are ignored. Investors who modify their reactions to extreme events in a more reflective fashion usually emerge in good shape from major shocks.

In the days that followed September 11, shares plunged worldwide, with investors in the United States pulling approximately $29.5 billion out of their share funds in panic. Five days later, however, the S&P 500 enjoyed its second largest one-day gain of the year. Within a month it had risen 3.7 percent, rewarding investors who held firm. It is often said that there are only two problems with attempting to time markets: getting in and getting out. The evidence from history is that this simply doesn't work.

The Impact of a Short Memory

We also tend to place more emphasis on things that happened last week than those that happened last year. Obviously, if your divorce came through last week, as opposed to five years ago, it would be more likely to have an impact on decisions today.

The key factor behind the behavioral phenomenon known as *recency* is when the event happened rather than how big it was. This makes it difficult for investors to place short-term events in the long-term context of their overall strategies. Combined with immediate experience, just like saliency it can cause investors to overreact and to abandon sensible strategies at the wrong time.

"I Found It, So It Must Be Important"

Investors also overemphasize the value of information that is easily accessible, rather than searching out alternative sources. This has been labeled *availability bias*.

In researching *Beyond Greed and Fear*, Dr. Shefrin posed this question to a number of men and women: "What is the more frequent cause of death in the United States, homicide or stroke?"

Most people answered this question, he found, by seeing how many events in each category came to mind. If people recall more incidences of homicide than of stroke, as anyone who watches the evening news will surely do, they will probably answer that it causes more deaths. Similarly, doctors who work with stroke patients will almost certainly answer that stroke is the more dangerous. They are right. Stroke accounts for eleven times more deaths than do murders. Rather than accepting readily available information, we should be ready to perform rigorous research or enlist the help of those who do.

We are also influenced by the information that is placed directly in front of us at the time of our decision. Behavioral finance leaders Thaler and Benartzi, whom we introduced in earlier chapters, found that when presented with a list of available options, investors often diversified their portfolios simply by allocating funds equally across options. For example, if a pension fund offers its members seven share-based portfolios and two fixed-interest funds, investors are more likely to end up with a large allocation to shares, whether or not this suits their objectives. The range of funds offered, and the way in which they are presented to investors, can have a potentially striking impact on the construction of a portfolio.

HOW ANCHORING CAN LEAD YOU ASTRAY

Anchoring is a behavioral trait of which most professional negotiators, including your local real estate agent, are keenly aware. It is widely used across different forms of marketing, and like most mental mistakes, can cause us to lose perspective. Any advertisement that follows the simple formula "recommended retail price $50, now $30—save $20," is attempting to influence our judgment by using an initial anchor price of $50 to show what a good deal is being offered.

How would your response to such an advertisement differ if it merely stated the price as "now $30"? The chances are your anchor would be $30 and the price would seem neither a bargain nor overly expensive.

The technique is used extensively by real estate agents, who, when observing a potential buyer's interest in a property, will casually mention that the vendor is looking for a price a good 10–20 percent above what the agent knows the vendor will probably accept and what the real market value is.

Anchoring in Investment Markets

Investors in other markets may similarly become anchored to prices of assets, such as individual shares or entire markets, and vulnerable to misjudgments about the future. Say a well-known stock has traded at around $30 for three consecutive years. A temporary drop in earnings takes the market by surprise and the price falls to $25, with no major change in fundamentals. Investors anchored to the $30 starting price may well consider the stock a "buy," because it now looks relatively cheap. However, by any objective measure, it may still be worth much less than $25.

In investment markets, anchoring compounds other mental mistakes, such as investors' tendencies to be overconfident. In a rising stock market, for example, investors tend to assume that current stock prices are roughly fair value, and each new market high becomes an anchor against which subsequent highs are judged.

Anchoring is really what market commentators are describing when they refer to the "crucial" 12,000- or 13,000-point barriers for the Dow Jones Industrial Average. There is no reason for 12,000 or 13,000 points on the Dow to have any greater significance than 11,993 or 12,331 points, yet these levels are recognized as psychologically important. Below 12,000 is "low," and above 12,000 is "fair value" or "high," until the market advances to its next anchor.

Anchoring plays a role in portfolio construction too, in particular the willingness of investors to take on a larger allocation to such growth assets as shares and property, where this is justified.

A long-term investor, with an ultraconservative portfolio heavy in cash and bonds, may be more willing to move to a greater weighting of shares incrementally over time, rather than all at once. It is easier to move to a 30 percent equity rating once the investor has become comfortable with a 20 percent weighting.

The same is true of the increasing tendency to invest offshore. For American investors who have traditionally exhibited a strong bias toward American investments, the shift overseas has been incremental. The same is true in most other major markets.

REFLECTIONS: Think back to the last time you bought a major asset such as an investment property or a new car. What were the stages of negotiation? Did you achieve a good deal? How do you know?

"Can't You See How Smart I Am?"

Anchoring is made worse by the propensity for investors to be excessively confident of their abilities, particularly if they have enjoyed recent success. Overconfidence often leads to poor decisions.

It explains why, for example, most people believe they are above average at everyday tasks like driving a car, when this is statistically impossible. Clearly, not everyone can be better than average.

Psychologists believe that overconfidence is more common than most of us care to admit. One of the reasons for this is that people tend to recall their successes more easily than their failures.

The ability to look on the bright side is a precondition for human development, as it seems unlikely we would have achieved so much if failures had loomed larger than successes. But confidence is clearly a positive influence only until it becomes excessive. The more difficult the task—for example, selecting a quality share portfolio—the greater the likelihood that overconfidence will play a role.

So how can you tell if your confidence level is justified? There is really no way of knowing, which highlights the vital role objective advice and constant self-monitoring should play in your financial strategies.

Overconfidence contributes to the tendency of many investors to

- Try to do it themselves, without the necessary skills and experience.
- Make decisions too rapidly, without sufficient analysis.
- Fail to diversify portfolios sufficiently.
- Trade investments too frequently.

TRADING TOO MUCH IS A WEALTH HAZARD

Excessive trading is one of the most destructive by-products of overconfidence. While many of those new to investing believe that frenetic activity and constant portfolio switches are keys to success, the evidence supports the opposite view.

On analyzing trading records for ten thousand accounts at a large discount brokerage house, University of California finance professor

Terrance Odean found that, on average, the securities that traders bought failed to make enough profit to cover transaction costs. They also performed worse than those securities the traders sold: traders sold winners and bought losers.

These findings tally with a report published by the North American Securities Administrators Association in August 1999, just six months before the peak of the technology-stock bubble. At the time, with markets soaring, it was widely perceived that day-trading was a way to make easy money. But while some did exceptionally well, the report found that 70 percent of Internet day traders in the United States were losing money. Even worse, most of these would "almost certainly lose everything they invest." And this finding was before the technology-stock bubble burst.

Investors with easy access to online share trading are like gamblers with access to roulette tables. While overconfidence in a market such as property can be a risk, property transactions take time, allowing investors to consider their actions. For share traders, the advent of real-time Internet transactions means that overconfidence can be acted upon within seconds.

Marketers understand this. The inference drawn from the image of a baby seated in front of a computer screen in an advertisement is clear: it's so easy, even a kid can do it. Advertising reinforces the misconception that information at your fingertips is the only ingredient necessary for success. The vital ingredient is not information, but understanding.

How to Lose Money Online

Odean and fellow University of California finance professor Brad Barber found that investors who had recently done well from shares and then moved their activities online traded stocks more frequently, speculated more, and achieved lower returns.

The researchers compared the investment performance of 1,607 investors who switched from telephone to online trading between 1991 and 1996 with the results of investors who did not switch. Their results were startling. They found that while those who moved online during the period had beaten the market by 2 percent before they went there, after the move their returns lagged behind the market by more than 3 percent (see figure below).

Odean and Barber suggest that the excessive trading that resulted from moving online was more than a response to lower trading costs and faster processing. Instead, they conclude that it is the nature of investing through the Internet that leads "gun" investors to trade too much. The Internet enables them to act too easily on overconfidence. They become victims of their own success.

Key offenders were likely to fit a risk taker's profile: young men with high incomes and a preference for small-company growth stocks with high market risk.

It is probably no coincidence that this profile is similar to that of many drivers who cause car accidents: overconfident young men.

Why Men Are the Biggest Losers

Studies in general psychology have consistently shown that men are generally more confident than women. As a result, men trade stocks more than women do, and so achieve worse investment performance.

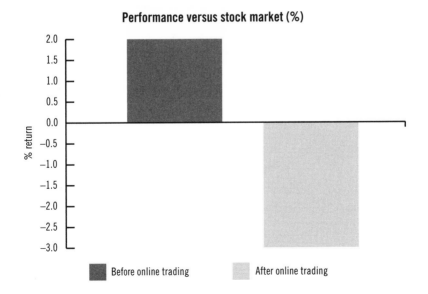

Performance versus stock market (%)

Further research by Odean and Barber, using account data on more than thirty five thousand households from February 1991 to January 1997, and analyzing the stock investments of both men and women, found that men traded 45 percent more than women did. What's more, this reduced men's net returns by 2.65 percent annually, compared to a reduction of 1.72 percent annually for women. Women perform better than men because of their *behavior*. It has nothing to do with the performance of the markets.

The High Price of a High IQ

While young male risk takers are among those most likely to pay a price for overconfidence, they are not the only group. Intelligent professionals, such as engineers, business managers, and doctors, are notoriously poor investors, often because they assume that success in their own discipline will translate seamlessly to the investment arena. They will rarely devote the time to study the market they have to achieving eminence in their professions.

Many financial advisers will tell you that well-educated clients are the most prone to poor decisions. It is far from unusual to hear of specialist physicians who have blown their savings on the latest get-rich-quick scheme. Decisions based on intuition can have unexpected outcomes, and high-IQ individuals are often more likely to act on intuition, to their detriment.

We have already seen how Sir Isaac Newton, one of the greatest human minds of all time, was caught up in one of the most extraordinary stock market bubbles in history. He did not have the discipline to master the feelings of envy that arose when he witnessed people far less intelligent than himself enjoying far greater success.

A PRACTICAL GUIDE TO BEATING MISTAKES

Let's now look at the practical steps you can take to guard against the mental mistakes described in this chapter.

The first and most important way to protect against mental mistakes is to have a sound investment framework, based on what we call the Four Golden Principles: Quality, Value, Diversity, Time (see the figure below).

Investing in Quality investments at prices that represent good Value in a Diverse range and for sufficient Time is a reliable way to build wealth.

Portfolios based on these principles sometimes deliver lower returns for a period, but they rarely result in permanent capital loss and have a more reliable long-term payoff.

During the technology-stock bubble of the late 1990s, the global technology sector returned 60 percent to investors in 1998 alone, and rose 130 percent more to the peak of the market in March 2000, as measured by the Nasdaq Composite Index.

This bubble surpassed even the "Nifty Fifty" growth stocks of the early 1970s, when investors treated companies like Kodak, Avon, and Xerox as stocks you could buy and hold forever. This worked perfectly until stagflation and recession set in and these stocks fell 46 percent in 1973–74. Some lost 80 percent of their value.

Three years later, not one Nifty Fifty stock had recovered, and they underperformed for the rest of the decade.

Many portfolios that focused on the Nifty Fifty in the 1970s or the global technology sector in the 1990s recorded real and permanent losses. They didn't understand the meaning of Quality and Value.

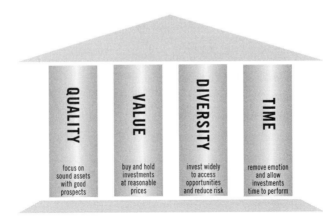

HOW QUALITY, VALUE, DIVERSITY, AND TIME WORK

Quality

The only way to identify quality companies is through rigorous analysis— and even professional analysts don't always get it right.

First, there is always a clear reason why quality companies make profits and pay dividends, and do so consistently. They are not slaves to market fashion.

Quality companies may range from new players with fresh ideas to well-established concerns. Typical attributes include sound longer-term earnings potential; good return on equity; capable management with a solid track record; a sound balance sheet; and reliable core business franchises. They can be household names like Coca-Cola or American Express, or smaller and relatively little-known companies.

Quality companies, bought at the right price, will generally get through even a severe market downturn.

REFLECTIONS: Do you hold quality investments in your portfolio? How do you know?

Value

The second principle of sensible investing, Value, is a function of quality and price.

Recall the example of Elizabeth and Sebastian Worthington from chapter 1, whose strategy required London property prices to keep on rising. The apartment they paid for may have been excellent and built of quality materials—but the Value was missing.

Some of the worst disasters have arisen from people paying too much for what are, essentially, quality assets.

Entrepreneur Alan Bond, who led the syndicate that wrested the America's Cup from the New York Yacht Club in 1983, learned this the hard way. In the mid-1980s, he bought Australia's Nine TV Network from media mogul Kerry Packer for a huge sum. Within a few short years, he sold it back to Packer for a fraction of the price. The Nine TV Network was a quality company, both when Bond bought it and when he sold it. The difference was that Packer better understood its Value, and this understanding helped him to become one of the world's richest people.

The key to assessing Value and Quality is to know whether an asset can produce an attractive return, relative to its risk. Professional fund managers usually have the ways and means to identify these attributes.

Diversity

Diversification involves having investments across different asset classes, countries, and funds.

While many people start investing in a diversified portfolio, they typically end up keeping investments that have delivered the best returns and weeding out those that have delivered low returns. They are often left with a portfolio of overvalued assets, which is then highly vulnerable to a market downturn. The subprime mortgage crisis that started in 2007 and coincided with a large rise in energy prices saw investors abandon financial stocks and simultaneously push energy stocks to record levels. Investors whose portfolios have excessive exposure to a sector like energy stocks, no matter how good its recent performance, are taking a big risk.

Diversification involves holding a wide range of investments and provides insurance against mistakes in assessing Value.

Not all successful investors diversify widely: Warren Buffett, for example, showed that focused portfolios could pay off. However, investors such as Buffett typically have access to significant analytical resources and also use direct intervention techniques such as buying controlling stakes in companies and changing their management when necessary. This type of success is rare.

Buffett biographer James O'Loughlin observes, "When Buffett can effectively 'eliminate' risk through objective and exhaustive analysis of the price/value equation then he selects only a few investments. Where the quantification of risk is necessarily subjective, he diversifies."

For those keen to be actively involved in the stock market with at least part of their portfolio, an effective approach may be to invest core wealth in a widely diversified, professionally managed portfolio. With the remainder of your wealth, define a narrow circle of competence, and invest in a concentrated portfolio of shares that fall into this circle and meet the criteria for Quality and Value.

Time

The ultimate test of a successful portfolio comes with Time.

While the first three of the Four Golden Principles were not fully rewarded in the late 1990s, they reemerged with the collapse of the technology-stock bubble. Investors who focused on such stocks achieved bumper returns in the late 1990s, followed by a catastrophic crash and then a marginal recovery.

Investors who focused on the broader stock market still suffered during one of the worst bear markets in history, but the pain was far less severe and the recovery far swifter.

Over virtually all longer periods in markets, say five to ten years or more, strategies based on the Four Golden Principles have greater upside potential, with less downside risk, than chasing fads. However, it's essential to ensure that the Four Golden Principles continue to be applied rigorously, and it's important to play an active role in monitoring your portfolio.

Since it's essential to take a long-term view, develop a plan that takes into account your entire investment time horizon rather than focuses on

Portfolios Based on the Four Golden Principles

Outperform when	Underperform when
Markets are "normal"	Markets are distorted
Quality is driving markets	Speculation or fear is driving markets
Returns are from diverse stocks	Returns are highly concentrated
Shares are assessed on merit	Shares are assessed on excessive "blue sky," or excessive gloom

the return in your latest portfolio report. The long term is made up of lots of short terms, one after another. Some of them will be good, others bad, but it's only the trend over time you need to worry about.

Consider not just the level of returns when reviewing your portfolio report but how these returns were generated. For example, if returns were sky-high, but a large proportion of the portfolio was invested in one stock, consider how sustainable this performance will be. A sudden fall in the stock that was driving returns may leave you high and dry.

Instill automatic discipline into your investment strategy to help avoid knee-jerk reactions to new circumstances. Commit to a regular savings plan whereby a set amount of money is automatically invested each month, irrespective of market conditions.

Similarly, set your portfolio so that it rebalances periodically between the various asset classes. This means that when shares have been particularly strong relative to other investments you own, you automatically reduce your holdings slightly; when shares have been weak, you increase your holdings. This way you increase your chances of buying low and selling high. The key here is automation, which reduces the risk that behavioral biases will lead to poor decisions.

Read widely to ensure your exposure to a variety of investment perspectives. This will help to reduce your vulnerability to the availability bias—"I read it in the paper so it must be true"—and allow you to gain a broader perspective on major events such as September 11. If you read what everyone else reads, you will probably think what everyone else thinks.

Use a financial adviser as an objective guide to help you manage your responses to changes in markets and investment conditions. Someone who can help you address such issues as overconfidence and anchoring, which are very difficult to address alone, will help you avoid poor decisions. In chapter 12 we'll look at some of the helpful characteristics to look for in a financial adviser.

LEARN FROM THE MONEY MASTERS

A smart way to gain perspective is to review the insights and actions of those who have achieved success. As we've mentioned earlier, one of the great masters is American investor Warren Buffett, the second wealthiest person in the world.

The Buffett Approach to Investment

Perhaps the best news for us about Buffett is that his success has been due largely to his *behavior* rather than to *exceptional intelligence*, something which is rather harder to replicate. He is humble, sensible and thrifty, well grounded, and disciplined. He is clear about the nature of risk and return in investment markets and about his goals. He does not appear to be distracted by others' expectations, excessive materialism, shortcuts to wealth, and the myriad other urgent but unimportant distractions. While there are countless books on Buffett's investment prowess, few observe the real key to his success: his behavior in life and behavior with money are entirely consistent. As Roger Lowenstein observes in his biography of Buffett, "Most of what Buffett did was imitable by the average person . . . His genius was largely a genius of character—of patience, discipline and rationality."

Buffett uses three main techniques to overcome the challenges described in this chapter.

1. Reframe the way the market works, and consider volatility as a friend that provides opportunities.

2. Undertake rigorous analysis on companies within your circle of competence before making decisions.

3. Have a reasonable expectation of performance, remain patient, and avoid the distractions of greed and peer pressure.

TREAT MR. MARKET'S VOLATILITY AS A FRIEND   In volatile times, it is said that, "wealth transfers from weak hands to strong hands." We have already seen how behavior has the biggest impact on investment results, and the ability to capture the Investment Prize. Buffett's positive attitude and behavior are pivotal to his success.

Buffett draws on Benjamin Graham's Wall Street character, Mr. Market, to explain his approach to the stock market. This personification of the stock market is a powerful illustration of the way Buffett uses analogies to demystify what many would see as shocking and scary behavior. In so doing, it allows him to see opportunities where others see problems and to remain disciplined in his own behavior, even in the extremes of market panic, such as in October–November 2008.

In *The Essays of Warren Buffett*, compiled by Lawrence Cunningham, Buffett asks us to imagine market quotations coming from Mr. Market, a remarkably acommodating fellow who acts as your partner on the stock market. Buffett points out that Mr. Market appears daily and names a price at which he will either buy your intrest or sell you his. And regardless of how stable the business that you may own is, Mr. Market's quotations will be anything but, because he has incurable emotional problems.

> At times [Mr. Market] feels euphoric and can see only the favorable factors affecting the business. When in that mood, he names a very high buy-sell price because he fears that you will snap up his interest and rob him of imminent gains. At other times he is depressed and can see nothing but trouble ahead for both the business and the world. On these occasions he will name a very low price, since he is terrified that you will unload your interest on him.

Mr. Market now seems quite endearing rather than frightening, and all the more so when Buffett points out that Mr. Market doesn't mind being ignored. Transactions are always purely at your option, and if you don't like his quotation today, he will be back with a new one tomorrow. So while most people are scared by volatility, Buffett points out that the more manic-depressive the behavior of Mr. Market is, the better it is for you.

STAY WITHIN THE CIRCLE OF COMPETENCE   Buffett started his investment career by studying share price charts. He dabbled with technical analysis, was receptive to hot tips, and produced ordinary results.

His turning point was learning from Graham how to apply fundamental mathematical discipline to valuing shares. Buffett's focus today is on buying shares in companies that are worth more than he pays for them.

The concept is simple enough, but the calculation of intrinsic value is difficult since it involves forecasting the future.

Buffett, as chairman of Berkshire Hathaway Corporation, and Charles Munger, as vice chairman, deal with this challenge in two ways. First, they stick to businesses they understand. "You don't have to be an expert on every company, or even many," Buffett said in a 1996 letter to Berkshire Hathaway shareholders. "You only have to be able to evaluate companies in your circle of competence. The size of that circle is not very important: knowing its boundaries, however, is vital."

Buffett's main focus, under the influence of Munger, is to concentrate on businesses that have great and enduring franchises and are led by outstanding managers. These businesses are usually relatively simple.

As Buffett disarmingly admitted in another letter to Berkshire Hathaway shareholders in 1992, "If a business is complex or subject to constant change, we're not smart enough to predict future cash flows. We are searching for operations that we believe are virtually certain to possess enormous competitive strength ten or twenty years from now. A fast-changing industry environment may offer the chance for huge wins, but it precludes the certainty we seek . . . I would rather be certain of a good result than hopeful of a great one."

Second, Buffett has persisted with Graham's key concept to insist on a margin of safety in the price paid. If their firm calculates the value of a share to be only slightly higher than its price, Buffett and Munger won't buy. They believe this margin of safety to be the cornerstone of investment success.

These factors provide Buffett with an emotional buffer against the behavior of the herd. They also provide the confidence not to worry about major political or economic events that may cause disruption, sometimes for prolonged periods, but ultimately don't affect the Investment Prize.

Buffett puts it bluntly in his annual report of 1995: "We will continue to ignore political and economic forecasts, which are an expensive distraction for many investors and businessmen."

In the years that we have followed the fortunes of the global economy and investments, markets have experienced major shocks that no one could have foreseen: the stagflation (high inflation combined with recession) that followed the trebling in oil prices in the 1970s; oil prices then fluctuating over the next thirty years between highs of more than $150 and lows of $10; the collapse of the Soviet Union and the replacement of the Cold War with the War on Terror; interest rates fluctuating between 2 and almost 20 percent; major booms and collapses in the bond, property, and stock markets; the subprime mortgage crisis that began in 2007 and led to the global financial crisis of 2008; among others.

Yet, none of these events has undermined the long-term value of the Investment Prize or the Four Golden Principles.

In the midst of the financial turmoil in 2008, Buffett put his money where his mouth was by investing heavily in U.S. shares. He challenged those who had retreated to the sidelines, saying in the New York Times on October 16, 2008 that cash equivalents were "a terrible long-term asset ... certain to depreciate in value." He maintained that equities would be the stronger performer over the next decade.

FURTHER READING FOR PART 2

IF YOU ARE INTERESTED IN UNDERSTANDING Buffett's investment process in more detail, we recommend these books.

Lawrence A. Cunningham's *The Essays of Warren Buffett: Lessons for Corporate America* organizes many of Buffett's major speeches and presentations in a single source.

Roger Lowenstein's *Buffett: The Making of an American Capitalist* is a more traditional biography.

James O'Loughlin's *The Real Warren Buffett: Managing Capital, Leading People* provides the most insightful and holistic analysis of what underpins Buffett's success.

Alice Schroeder's *The Snowball: Warren Buffett and the Business of Life*, which is the first authorized biography of the investor and philanthropist.

If you want to read what good financial advisers are reading about how to invest your money, two books, both edited by respected advisers Harold Evensky and Deena Katz, are a useful place to start: *The Investment Think Tank: Theory, Strategy, and Practice for Advisers* and *Retirement Income Redesigned: Master Plans for Distribution: An Adviser's Guide for Funding Boomers' Best Years*.

A number of well-known fund managers have been at the forefront of developing strategies that use insights from behavioral finance to identify shares that are too expensive or too cheap. More information on these strategies, for readers with a technical interest, is available from

www.barclaysglobal.com, which has a knowledge center with an array of research articles. Barclays Global Investors is one of the world's largest fund managers and has built a strong reputation for innovative yet disciplined quantitative research.

www.bernstein.com, which provides easy-to-read and insightful commentary from the AllianceBernstein investment powerhouse. Alliance is well known as one of the world's biggest "growth"-style investment managers, and Bernstein as one of the world's best "value"-style managers.

www.lsvasset.com, which provides links to a series of technical articles. LSV Asset Management was founded in 1994 by three professors in the fields of finance and economics—Josef Lakonishok, Andrei Shleifer, and Robert Vishny—all recognized for their work in behavioral finance.

PART 3

WEALTH AND WELL-BEING:

Your wealth creation strategy, and how it can contribute to your well-being

Chapter 12

GOOD AND BAD ADVISERS

ONE IMPORTANT DECISION THAT WE ALL MAKE is whether to build our Bridge of Well-being and manage our wealth habits by ourselves, to seek expert advice, or to do a bit of both. While everyone is different, it's smart to seek objective advice, at least as a sounding board for major financial decisions and to provide an objective, continuing assessment of our wealth habits.

Even if you have the technical abilities to implement your own wealth strategy, good financial advisers are like personal trainers. They can help you develop your financial strategy, monitor your portfolio, and make sure it continues to support your plans for the future.

In short, financial advisers have the ability and are trained to play a valuable and constructive role in contributing to your wealth and well-being and helping you to achieve the Ultimate Prize.

However, it's important to recognize that, because financial advising is still a relatively new profession, standards vary. Too many advisers focus purely on selling financial products because they are rewarded solely by commissions linked to the volume of transactions they make.

While qualifications, standards, and professionalism in the industry are improving steadily, consistent quality advice is not yet the norm. You need to find the right adviser for your life.

GOOD ADVISERS

There are six key credentials and attributes to look for in a financial adviser.

1. The industry's highest technical qualification, a Certified Financial Planner. This should ensure adequate technical competence with respect to investments, tax, estate planning, insurance, budgeting, and other financial matters.

2. A broad education and a broad frame of reference and experience. A good adviser has the ability to apply mature judgment. It is your well-being that the adviser is dealing with, not merely your money, so you need someone who is not just a financial technician.

3. An intuitive and educated understanding of behavioral finance. You need someone who doesn't become a victim of the mental mistakes we have outlined. This is one of the most critical attributes, given the relative ease with which an astute adviser can put together a good quality portfolio.

4. A fee structure that minimizes any tendency toward biased recommendations. It is wise to avoid advisers who rely mainly on transaction-based commissions. Rather than helping you stick to your financial strategy in the face of market noise, such advisers may encourage you to trade regularly in order to increase their own paychecks. Be aware that different investment products pay different commissions, with the higher-risk products paying the largest. Pay a fee for the service you need. Generally, advisers who are remunerated primarily on the basis of fees for initial and continuing advice are less likely to encourage excessive trading. They are also less likely to prefer products that are worth more to their own financial positions than to yours.

5. Access to significant technical resources and a team to provide continuity of service, should your adviser decide to move on or to retire. While there are many good advisers, financial strategies are so complex that no one person can know everything. A good adviser is like a good general practitioner in medicine, with the ability to call in specialists as necessary. When the adviser is away (temporarily or permanently), you need to know who will be there to guide you

through the continuous changes, events, and crises that will occur, either in your life or in the markets.

6. A genuine sense of care. There is no one more dangerous than a highly intelligent person who cares only about him- or herself. A caring adviser will show an interest in you as a person, and go well beyond the money you have. Ask yourself whether the advice given is for you, the person, or for the money you bring.

REFLECTIONS: If you already have a financial adviser, think about whether you believe they genuinely plan for you as a person, rather than merely for your money.

BAD ADVISERS

Just as you can identify good financial advisers by the traits listed previously, you can spot bad advisers just as readily if any of the following ring true about someone you've hired or are thinking to hire. In general, bad financial advisers will

- Take credit for portfolio performance when markets go up, yet blame the markets during periods of weak performance.
- Confidently predict future market conditions using expressions such as "The market has peaked" or "The market has taken a dive."
- Never convey a genuine sense of understanding you as a person.
- Give you unrealistic expectations as to what is achievable, typically promising far too much.
- Switch and trade your portfolio constantly, or make sweeping adjustments without proper justification.
- Talk about investment returns as if they control the markets, rather than encouraging you to understand and manage risk.
- Be unable to explain why their recommendations are relevant to the lifestyle you want.

HOW TO FIND YOUR FINANCIAL SOUL MATE

Newspaper articles often publish lists of the questions you should ask a financial adviser to establish his or her credentials. Among such questions are

- What are your qualifications?
- Are you tied to the manufacturer of a particular product?
- How are you remunerated?
- What conflicts of interest might arise?

REFLECTIONS: What questions might you ask a prospective adviser to determine whether they are good or not? Would you consider asking to talk to some existing clients, to get a personal reference?

While it is essential to pose question such as these, they won't necessarily help you find the right adviser. You want someone with those magical ingredients of trust, competence, and empathy that will make a genuine difference to your life. From the start, it is vital to find someone you trust and with whom you feel comfortable sharing private information. You need to satisfy yourself that your trust is well founded.

What Should You Expect of a Financial Adviser?

A good adviser should assist you in six main ways.

1. Help you determine your goals by asking you the right questions and encouraging you to think carefully about your answers. A good adviser spends plenty of time listening and learning about you, your perceptions, experiences, feelings, and desires; he or she takes a personal interest in *you*.

2. Provide the tools and technical expertise to help link your goals to your financial resources, and help you identify your priorities and make informed choices. A good adviser helps you understand your

true needs and goals and provides continuing transparent advice about the performance of your investments and general financial position.

3. Enable you to access skills in financial strategy, economics, investments, taxation, estate planning, social security, and behavioral finance, and use these to develop a coherent financial plan. A good adviser explains ideas and conveys information confidently and clearly.

4. Add discipline to your investment approach so that you don't become a victim of "short-termism" and of following the latest trend. A good adviser helps you set clear benchmarks to measure both your success and his or hers; tempers your enthusiasm during periods when investments are performing extremely well; and boosts your confidence when your investments are performing poorly.

5. Provide a service throughout your lifetime to help you deal with changing personal and external circumstances, such as new legislation or tax rules. A good adviser will likewise challenge the status quo and encourage you to explore new horizons.

6. Assist you in developing the ability to avoid the mental mistakes and traps outlined in *How Much Is Enough?* This sometimes involves having the adviser play devil's advocate to help you assess the evidence objectively.

What Should Your Adviser Expect of You?

No matter how good your financial adviser, the success of your life plan ultimately depends on you. No coach can succeed with an athlete who lacks commitment. In the financial world, this requires a number of commitments from you.

- Take time to gain a basic understanding of the relationship between risk and return and be realistic about what you can expect from an investment. Don't expect your adviser to be able to generate large, risk-free gains for you, nor to predict the direction of investment markets. No adviser can do this. Ignore the advertisements and other noise that suggest this is somehow possible.

- Put serious effort into thinking through your signature strengths, goals, and priorities. In other words, decide what is truly important to you. This will critically influence your plan and, more importantly, the quality of your future life.

- Stay informed about what is happening in investment markets, and use this information to influence your expectations of portfolio reports. For example, if speculative companies soaring in value are dominating the headlines, then expect your portfolio to underperform in the market. If it outperforms during such a period, you should seriously question your adviser's competence. He or she just might have joined in the speculation with your hard-earned savings!

- Expect to pay for good advice. The best financial advisers are qualified professionals who deserve to be well paid for the services they provide. No true professional is going to provide free advice. Free advice is often worth what you paid for it.

MEET THE KUMARS

A good financial adviser can do a lot more than simply help you manage your money. He or she can actually help improve the quality of your life.

Such was the case for Fred Kumar, an American academic who had lived in Hong Kong and Singapore for two decades before returning to his native San Francisco. Fred was fond of saying that the best thing to come out of his time in Asia was his wife, Sui, an Asian teacher who had been educated in Australia.

By the time Fred was fifty, he and Sui were anticipating a relaxed and comfortable retirement together. Fred was earning $85,000 per annum, Sui $45,000, and they owned their apartment, appraised at $1.3 million. Their daughter, Ayesha, was about to graduate from medical school and move out on her own.

The Kumar family apartment was larger than they required, but it suited their financial strategy, which focused on property. It seemed obvious to Fred and Sui that people would always need homes, and husband and wife both believed they could easily trade down to a smaller place once they retired.

The stock market had not been kind. Fred had read the detailed analyses provided by his stockbroker, had bought into the market when sentiment was right, and had taken the advice of friends who assured him they always did well. Yet Fred suffered several spectacular failures. An unkind joke had emerged in the Kumar household. When Fred hit the market, you'd better stand back, because the "Kumar collapse" was on the way.

I can't really blame the stockbroker, thought Fred. He had given the Kumars good advice. They had held on, switched sectors, and tried concentrating on a handful of shares. This had resulted in a dizzying ride as the portfolio switched from technology stocks, to commodities, to health care and emerging markets. Yet nothing worked for long.

Fred had never really figured out the return on his share portfolio, but he had the uneasy feeling he'd be lucky to break even. Nevertheless, between their pension fund (invested in cash after their bad stock market experience) and other investments, the Kumars had saved almost $500,000. Their new car was also paid off.

Life looked pretty good. At home one evening, Fred and Sui reflected for the first time on plans for their retirement. "I'll be ready to put my feet up by sixty," said Fred. "We'll travel where we want, instead of where the business sends me." Sui, worn down by years in the school system, didn't take much convincing.

"We can probably live comfortably on $50,000 a year," Fred told her. "Our savings will see us out. We've also got to think about Ayesha's wedding, our travel plans, and leaving something for our grandchildren."

Because they were conservative at heart, Fred and Sui decided to schedule a quick checkup with a friend, Ellery, who was a qualified financial adviser, to review their plans and tie up any loose ends.

They were in for a shock.

After mapping their proposed lifestyle against their current financial resources, and keeping their investments in cash as requested, Ellery projected that the Kumars would run out of money by the time Fred was seventy one—a good twelve years short of his life expectancy and some eighteen years short of Sui's. What's more, there was little in reserve to pay for any major health crises or other unexpected expenses. Worse, with the anticipated influx of baby boomers to inner cities, the Kumars' "trade-down" strategy for their apartment might not free up nearly as much capital as expected. They might need to move farther out from the city, not farther in.

When Sui mentioned plans for her daughter's grand wedding, it was all Ellery could do to refrain from saying, "Let's hope she elopes!"

What Can the Kumars Do Now?

The Kumars appear to have it all. Their financial resources are significant, and their lifestyle aspirations are not particularly extravagant. And yet, like the average American couple, they face a major lifestyle crunch in retirement.

For them as well as for many other middle-class couples around the world, three factors have brought about their dilemma.

- Failing to understand how long people now live, and how to properly plan for this change.

- Investing too much in residential property, particularly the family home, without a realistic understanding of what cash will be freed up when it's traded down. This is a big problem for both baby boomers and Gen Xers.

- Failing to invest effectively for retirement over their working lives, and in particular, failing to capture the Investment Prize. Had they captured even an additional 3 percent on their pension and other investment assets over their working lifetimes, upon retirement the value of these would have almost doubled.

So, how do the millions of families who face the same challenge as the Kumars solve the problem? The worst approach is to automatically respond by putting money into the highest-yielding investments. In many cases, a funding gap cannot be closed by investment returns alone. This route often leads to damaging speculation and permanent loss.

FOCUS ON YOUR LIFE, NOT YOUR MONEY

Fortunately, and before it's too late for the Kumars, they have asked the right questions. By making a variety of relatively small compromises, and by managing their money more effectively, they can still achieve much of what they hope for. They don't need to take big investment risks or see their key hopes dashed but, rather, to focus on developing plans that reflect their true spending habits and making some simple choices to suit their preferences.

These decisions include

- Increasing their savings once their daughter graduates and leaves home. Many couples at this stage of their lives, as their children become less dependent, find they are able to increase their savings substantially. The best way to do this is to save the extra income before it is even received.

- Updating their car every six to seven years, rather than every five years. This will have little if any impact on their well-being but will save them thousands of dollars, a classic example of hedonic arbitrage (maintaining happiness while spending less).

- Reducing their spending from age seventy, as age begins to restrict activity. Going on less-expensive vacations would also help. Instead, they could focus on a couple of luxury world trips.

Taking these actions would extend the Kumars' money for an extra three years, still well short of their expectations. They considered further. The couple found that if Fred works for an extra three years, and they further trim their expenditure after age seventy five, this would add another five years to the life of their funds, thus extending the life of their capital by almost a decade in total.

Finally, if in addition they invest their savings more effectively, and capture an extra 3 percent annually in a growth portfolio while Fred is still working, and then an extra 1 percent each year in a more defensive growth portfolio after he retires, the couple's funds will last well into their nineties.

Their comfort, peace of mind, and ability to deal with crises in retirement will be substantially increased. And Sui's desire to have something left for future grandchildren will be realized. This could hold true for you as well.

Chapter 13

HOW MUCH IS ENOUGH?

ALMOST DAILY, NEWSPAPERS REPORT STORIES of those who have lost their life savings through bad decisions in the stock market or through property scandals, or who have fallen prey to other schemes and scams that lie in wait for the unwary. The stories are different, but the results are the same: always a tragedy, and almost always avoidable.

For every story of failure, however, there is another possible version: an alternative history, if you will.

AN ALTERNATIVE HISTORY FOR THE WORTHINGTONS

Recall from chapter 1 the example of Elizabeth and Sebastian Worthington, the London-based couple whose marriage was put under extreme pressure by Sebastian's speculation on the property market. First, it's important to recognize that the Worthingtons' real challenge was lifestyle, not money. Sebastian was working long hours away from home, and Elizabeth was under pressure with their young family. The more family-friendly environment that their renovation would create seemed the answer to all their problems. And perhaps it was.

Suppose that instead of going to Sebastian's colleagues, the couple had discussed their plans with a financial adviser. An adviser with his eyes on sales commissions might have focused on investment, waxed lyrical on prospects for the property market, made some forecasts, and concluded with something like: "Well, it's probably a good investment, but I can recommend something that will suit you even better." Such an approach exploits all the behavioral weaknesses of the Worthingtons in order to sell a financial product.

A financial adviser or coach of the type described in the last chapter, however, may have declined to discuss the investment and focused instead on what was motivating the Worthingtons to consider such a risk. Bearing in mind that the couple had a lifestyle problem, rather than a financial one, a good adviser may have encouraged them to consider alternatives to renovating their home. They could move to a different area, bring in extra support from family and friends, or engage a nanny. Maybe Sebastian could change jobs.

In other words, a good financial adviser would have focused on helping the couple to achieve the Ultimate Prize by maximizing their well-being, as well as improving their financial prospects. Such an adviser would have used the concept of hedonic arbitrage to reframe the couple's thinking and help them see the need to maximize happiness rather than to focus on money alone.

With a full picture of their lifestyle and aspirations, a good adviser would have presented the Worthingtons with the realistic choices and probable outcomes of any investment strategy. Armed with this information, they would have been able to make a more informed choice than taking a risk on property.

Really good advice may have sounded something like this:

> People have made quick profits recently buying property, but you need to understand that this is speculating on the property cycle. No one can predict exactly what will happen, and it's not something I can advise you on with any confidence.
>
> What I can do is look at the implications of the risks and returns of this investment and what the investment could mean for your lifestyle. If it pays off, you might make around £100,000 over two years, enough to pay for your renovation—and then some. But that still won't make you

rich, and the chances of getting this result are less than 25 percent. In other words, it's possible, but not likely.

On the other hand, there's a 25 percent chance you'll miss the property cycle and end up losing money—or even having to borrow to buy the apartment and ride out the cycle. If this happens, you would have to postpone your house renovations for at least five years, and this seems likely to reduce your enjoyment of home life.

Given the importance of the renovation to Elizabeth's peace of mind, these odds don't seem very attractive. Do you really want to take the risk?

The Worthingtons may have then been able to develop a budget and allocate their savings into pools, such as

- A money market account, to pay for short-term goals

- A fixed-term deposit, or defensive fund, for the medium term

- A growth portfolio for the longer term, taking advantage of the tax-effective nature of pension funds

Had Elizabeth and Sebastian taken this advice, they could have avoided the disaster that befell them, and other pitfalls discussed throughout *How Much Is Enough?* Today they would be enjoying a better life. It is clear from this case study that there is a direct correlation between financial decisions and personal well-being.

HOW MUCH IS ENOUGH?

If you've read up to this point, it means that you're serious about trying to achieve the Ultimate Prize. Learning to maximize your happiness for any given level of wealth lies at the heart of solving the enigmatic question "How much *is* enough?" But the value of this knowledge will be in the doing, not the reading. What actions you take immediately after finishing this book will help to determine your level of wealth and happiness for the rest of your life. Please read this section carefully.

If your life to date has not been especially happy, you may have too often been distracted from doing what is really important to you. You may have been caught up in the business of day-to-day life, where an astonishing number of things (mobile phone calls, e-mails, text messages, and other urgent but ultimately unimportant tasks) clamor for attention. Peer pressure, exacerbated by excessive attention to material values, is a more insidious cause of unease. Such pressures, which undermine our ability to capture the Investment Prize, further undermine our well-being and reduce our financial security.

To understand how easy it is to let time slip through your fingers without creating any abiding feelings of satisfaction, take a few minutes to do the following exercise.

Relax, close your eyes, and spend a few minutes recalling all the *truly happy* memories that you have from the past five years. When you're ready, open your eyes. If the time seemed to fly by, but instead of five minutes you spent twenty to thirty minutes in joyful recollection of abundant happy memories, then read no further. The chapters of our book on wealth creation may be useful for you, but you have already achieved a high degree of well-being.

For most people, however, this exercise takes a much shorter time. They start to fidget after a few minutes, their minds start to wander to more pressing and mundane issues, and they find it difficult to recall episodes of true happiness. Imagine not being able to easily fill our minds with even a few minutes of happy memories of the past five years! If you do nothing about rebalancing the attention you give to the important, as distinct from the urgent distractions in your life, then nothing will change for you. For most of us, this is a sobering thought. So, what will you commit to changing? What's really important to you?

To define this is one of the most important things you can do to make a real difference in your life. To gain perspective, retry an exercise we recommended earlier in the book, giving it your full attention. Imagine your closest friend giving a speech at your funeral about what you have achieved in your life. Write it down. You may wish to compile a simple list, or you may want to use phrases or even continuous prose to draw out your thoughts.

Here's an example that draws on real-life experiences. Bernie Fernando's life took a major turn when, at the age of forty five, the company he had worked for all his life closed down. This company had been the biggest employer in town and was where Bernie's father and grandfather had worked. Upon hearing the news, Bernie felt a sense of despair and insecurity. How could he pay for his children's last few years of school, complete the mortgage payments, and fund his retirement?

The outplacement service provided by his employer was so concerned about his state of mind that they referred him to a psychologist. This helped, and Bernie's outlook improved.

On reflection, he realized that while his job had provided a sense of security, he had never much liked being cooped up in an office. He was an outdoors person with a passion for gardening. In a flash of insight, Bernie saw that by buying a franchise for a nursery, he could make a living out of his passion—a notion that being a "company man" had previously crushed. He now saw that he had been living his father's dream, not his own.

Bernie also found that his wife, Jenny, had a flair for business, and working in partnership with her freed him to concentrate on his passion for tending plants. Rather than contenting himself with sales, Bernie would visit customers building new houses or renovating their existing homes and advise them on the best plants to buy and where to position them.

He loved driving visitors around town, showing them the gardens he had helped to create, observing the children playing in them and feeling this was his way of making a contribution to the environment. His passion for his work, aided by Jenny's business skills, paid off commercially too. The extra service he provided allowed him to charge a premium for his plants, and customers bought more.

Best of all, his relationship with Jenny, which had been stale, flourished, greatly improving family life. Their eldest son, Shaun, went on to manage his own nursery franchise.

While the additional wealth they made from the business made life more comfortable, it also allowed the couple to support a cause that was important to them. Their first child, a daughter, had died of complications stemming from juvenile diabetes. After hours, Bernie and Jenny would tirelessly attend fundraisers, spend time with medical researchers deciding on the most promising research areas to fund, and support families with children afflicted by the disease.

Said Shaun at Bernie's funeral: "Dad got great pleasure from being outdoors, a sense of gratification from helping to build gardens. And he had a wonderful family life. What gave his life real meaning was the work he did for children with juvenile diabetes. Ironically, none of these things would have happened had he not been downsized, and his comfortable, secure world taken away from him."

Many similar stories have emerged from the town where Bernie spent his life, highlighting how difficult times can sometimes be the catalyst for a change for the better.

YOUR GOOD LIFE

It is important not to wait for tough times before you take action to steer your life in the right direction. Therefore, we offer these steps for you to consider now so that the next time you try to recall happy memories, you are overwhelmed by them. These steps will ensure that your eulogy reflects someone who led the good life, and that you are living a life that you want to lead rather than someone else's idea of how things should be.

- Make sure that your job gives you real satisfaction. For those of us in the workforce, the majority of our conscious hours are spent at work. Does your current job help you realize your own goals and values? If not, why not? Can you reexamine and reinterpret it so that it makes you feel better? Remember that the most basic job can give such satisfaction if you put your heart into it.

- Spend some time now thinking about your current job. If your cell phone rang immediately with a distant acquaintance wanting to have a chat, chances are you'd pick it up. Don't. This exercise is more important to your long-term happiness (although relationships are important too, so make sure you call your friend back later!).

- Remember to apply your signature strengths in the key areas of work, love, and raising children. This applies to many other areas of your life as well, but concentrate on these especially. Please visit our website, www.howmuchisenough.net, for more information on this important concept.

- Spend time thinking about what gives you a sense of gratification. Recall that gratifications typically involve skill, and they draw on your signature strengths to pursue activities that completely absorb you. They give you a sense of flow.

- Plan your time to maximize the gratifications. This will include work activities, which provide this feeling, mixed with pleasures in between. Don't spend most of your time on pleasures, with only the occasional gratification mixed in. Understanding this is a key to achieving the Happiness Prize.

- Remember to distinguish among long-, medium-, and short-term goals. Because it can be hard to be sure what goals will have the greatest positive effect, "try before you buy." Interviewing people who have experience in the goals that you wish to achieve is also a valuable source of information.

- Have a financial strategy for you, not just for your money. In other words, make sure that the key elements of your financial strategy— your level of savings, money behavior, spending patterns, the risks you take, and the overall investment approach—are all geared to help you achieve your goals. Too often, people make investments on an ad hoc basis because of tips, or simply having the opportunity placed in front of them, rather than as part of an overall strategy. The result is that their lifestyles end up being dictated by a series of random investment decisions instead of decisions geared to support their lifestyles.

- Capture the Investment Prize. Consider investing a significant proportion of your long-term savings in a globally diversified portfolio of shares to capture the Investment Prize. Remember that while the Investment Prize is not guaranteed, it has been reliable over long periods of time. The key reason why millions of people do not capture it is their own behavior. Apply the Four Golden Principles of Quality, Value, Diversity, and Time to ensure that your behavior is disciplined. Stay within your circle of competence. Draw on the knowledge you have gained from this book to understand how to avoid such mental mistakes as anchoring, saliency, representativeness, overconfidence, and relying on past performance. Recall that one of the biggest mistakes of the herd is to underinvest in shares and overinvest in property. Learn from their mistakes.

- Enlist the help of a competent and trustworthy financial adviser. It will be easy to recognize such a person. They will be able to explain their advice in words that resonate with who you are and what you want. They will not appeal to human greed and fear to make a sale. Rather, they will provide research, knowledge, and wisdom to help you strike the right balance and determine how much is enough.

THE FUTURE IS YOURS TO CONTROL

The first objective of *How Much Is Enough?* was to help you understand the tricks your mind plays that can cause a reduction in your financial resources and well-being. The second was to provide a range of strategies to help counter such mental mistakes, and to provide a framework, the Bridge of Well-being, to help you balance each decision against others. Our final goal was to challenge you to think about what will make your life happier and more meaningful.

Making the most of your financial resources, and effectively linking them to what you want from life, can help you develop the strength and ability to follow your own life course with greater confidence and peace of mind. Throughout *How Much Is Enough?* we have emphasized how wealth, your personal goals and values, and your well-being are all closely linked. The media is full of cautionary tales of the fall of financial gurus who understood everything about investment but little about what gives life meaning.

No single book can give meaning to our lives. That can come only from within. However, if we have encouraged you to really think hard about your life, and challenged you with the right questions, we will have succeeded in our most important goal. We hope that at the next barbecue with family and friends, when the talk turns to hot investment tips, you'll have the confidence not to join in the boasting. Recognize it for what it is, smile serenely, and change the subject to something more interesting.

Privately, you can luxuriate in one of the hardest feelings of all to achieve in a world of endless choice: a sense of control of your own destiny. A sense of knowing what you want, and why. A sense of knowing which course in life will maximize your happiness and allow you to experience the Ultimate Prize. A sense of knowing just how much is enough.

REFERENCES

Abey, Arun, Clifford German, and Ean Higgins. *Fortune Strategy*, London: Financial Times/Prentice Hall, 2001.

ABN AMRO/London Business School. *Global Investment Returns Yearbook 2008*. Accessed at www.abnamroresearch.com.

Antunovich, Peter, David Laster, and Scott Mitnick. "Are High-Quality Firms also High-Quality Investments?," *Current Issues in Economics and Finance* 6, no. 1 (Jan. 2000).

Barber, Brad M., and Terrance Odean. "All That Glitters: The Effect of Attention and News on the Buying Behavior of Individual and Institutional Investors," EFA 2005 Moscow Meetings Paper. 2006. Accessed at http://ssrn.com/abstract=460660.

———. "Online Investors: Do the Slow Die First?," *Review of Financial Studies* 15, no. 2 (2002): 455–89.

———. "The Courage of Misguided Convictions," *Financial Analysts Journal* 55, no. (Nov./Dec.1999): 41–55.

Barberis, Nicholas, Andrei Shleifer, and Robert Vishny. "A Model of Investor Sentiment." Working Paper. March 1998. Accessed at www.lsvasset.com.

Ben-Shahar, Tal. *Happier: Learn the Secrets to Daily Joy and Lasting Fulfillment*. New York: McGraw Hill, 2007.

Bearup, Greg. "Two of Us: Geoffrey Lee and Bilel Jideh." *Sydney Morning Herald (Good Weekend)*, May 6, 2006, 16.

Benartzi, Shlomo, and Richard H. Thaler. "Myopic Loss-Aversion and the Equity Premium Puzzle," *Quarterly Journal of Economics* 110, no. 1 (Feb. 1995): 73–92.

————. "Naïve Diversification Strategies in Defined Contribution Savings Plans" (Jan.1999). Accessed at www.fullerthaler.com/ResearchLibrary.

Bernoulli, Daniel. "Exposition of a New Theory on the Measurement of Risk," *Econometrica* 22 (1954): 23–36 (originally published in 1738).

Brock, Horace W. Research Report. Published in 2000 by Strategic Economic Decisions, Inc. (U.S.). Accessed at www.sedinc.com.

Buffett, Warren E. "Buy American, I Am," *New York Times*, Oct. 16, 2008.

Cairnes, Margot. *Staying Sane in a Changing World: A Handbook for Work, Leadership and Life in the 21st Century.* Pymble, NSW: Simon & Schuster Australia, 2003.

Campbell, John Y., Martin Lettau, Burton G. Malkiel, and Yexiao Xu. "Have Individual Stocks Become More Volatile? An Empirical Exploration of Idiosyncratic Risk," *Journal of Finance* LVI, no. 1 (Feb. 2001).

Carr-Gregg, Michael. *The Princess Bitchface Syndrome: Surviving Adolescent Girls.* Melbourne: Penguin, 2006.

Chancellor, Edward. *Devil Take the Hindmost: A History of Financial Speculation.* New York: Farrar, Straus & Giroux, 1999.

Cialdini, Robert B. *Influence: The Psychology of Persuasion*, rev. ed. New York: William Morrow, 1993.

Clitheroe, Paul. *Making Money: The Keys to Financial Success.* Melbourne: Viking, 2007.

Cox, Ken. "Daniel's Message for Doctors," *The Medical Journal of Australia* 178, no. 19 (May 2003): 510–11.

Croucher, John S. "Number Crunch," *Sydney Morning Herald (Good Weekend)*, Dec. 2, 2006, 11.

Csikszentmihalyi, Mihaly. *Finding Flow.* New York: Basic Books, 1997.

Cummins, Robert A., Jacqui Woerner, Adrian Tomyn, Adele Gibson, and T'Meika Knapp. "The Well-being of Australians—Income Security." Australian Unity Well-being Index Survey 15, Melbourne: Deakin University, 2006.

Cunningham, Lawrence A., ed. *The Essays of Warren Buffett: Lessons for Corporate America.* Durham, NC: Carolina Academic Press, 1998.

DALBAR Inc. *Quantitative Analysis of Investor Behavior: What Investors Really Do, What is in Their Best Interest and What It Costs Them.* 2006. Accessed at www.dalbarinc.com.

Daniel, Kent, and Sheridan Titman. "Market Efficiency in an Irrational World," *Financial Analysts Journal* (Nov./Dec. 1999): 28.

Dow Theory Letters, Oct. 26, 1994. Accessed at www.dowtheoryletters.com.

Dowrick, Stephanie. *Choosing Happiness: Life and Soul Essentials.* Australia: Allen & Unwin, 2006.

Duffy, Michael. "What Did They Know and … When Did They Know It?" *Time* (Jan. 28, 2002).

Eckersley, Richard. "Richer Is Better, Right? Well … No, Not Any More," *VicHealth Letter* 26 (Summer 2005).

"Economics Discovers Its Feelings—Not Quite as Dismal as It Was," *The Economist* (Dec. 23, 2006).

Ellis, Charles D. *Winning the Loser's Game: Timeless Strategies for Successful Investing,* 3rd ed. New York: McGraw-Hill, 1998.

Evensky, Harold, and Deena Katz, eds. *The Investment Think Tank: Theory, Strategy, and Practice for Advisers.* New York: Bloomberg, 2004.

———. *Retirement Income Redesigned: Master Plans for Distribution: An Adviser's Guide for Funding Boomers' Best Years.* New York: Bloomberg, 2006.

Eyre, Linda, and Richard Eyre. *Teaching Your Children Responsibility,* 1st Fireside ed., 1994.

Fisher, Kenneth L., and Meir Statman. "A Behavioral Framework for Time Diversification," *Financial Analysts Journal* (May/June 1999): 88.

Frankfurter, George M., and Elton G. McGoun. "Resistance Is Futile: The Assimilation of Behavioral Finance," *Journal of Economic Behavior and Organization* 48, no. 4 (2002): 375–89.

Fuller, Russell J. "Behavioral Finance and the Sources of Alpha," *Journal of Pension Plan Investing* 2 no. 3 (Winter 1998).

Gates, Bill and Melinda. www.gatesfoundation.org.

Gilbert, Daniel. *Stumbling on Happiness.* New York: Vintage Books, 2007.

Gittins, Ross. "Irrationalism Wins Credence," *Sydney Morning Herald,* Oct. 12–13, 2002.

———. "The Games That People Play," *Sydney Morning Herald,* June 10, 2000.

Goleman, Daniel. *Emotional Intelligence.* New York: Bantam Books, 1995.

Graham, Benjamin, and Jason Zweig. *The Intelligent Investor,* rev. ed. New York: Harper Business Essentials, 2003.

ipac Securities Limited. "The Loss of Control: A Snapshot of Australian Financial Security and Happiness." Research prepared by brandmanagement for ipac securities, March 2005. Accessed at www.ipac.com.au.

Jacobs, Gregg D. *The Ancestral Mind*. New York: Viking, 2003.

Jenkinson, Stephen. *Money and the Soul's Desires: A Meditation*. Toronto: Stoddart, 2002.

Kahneman, Daniel, and Mark W. Riepe. "Aspects of Investor Psychology," *Journal of Portfolio Management* 24 (1998): 52–65.

———. "Intuitive Prediction: Biases and Corrective Procedures." In D. Kahneman, P. Slovic, and A. Tversky, eds. *Judgement under Uncertainty: Heuristics and Biases*. Cambridge, UK: Cambridge University Press, 1982.

Kasser, Tim. *The High Price of Materialism*. Cambridge, Mass.: MIT Press, 2002.

Kidman, Antony D. *From Thought to Action*, 2nd ed. Sydney, Australia: Biochemical and General Services, 2001.

Kindleberger, Charles P. *Manias, Panics and Crashes: A History of Financial Crises*, 4th ed. New York: John Wiley & Sons, 2000.

Lacayo, Richard, and Amanda Ripley. "Persons of the Year: Cynthia Cooper, Coleen Rowley and Sherron Watkins," *Time* (Dec. 22, 2002).

Lifson, Lawrence E., and Richard A. Geist, eds. *The Psychology of Investing*. New York: John Wiley & Sons, 1999.

Lowenstein, Roger. *Buffett: The Making of an American Capitalist*. New York: Main Street Books, 1996.

Maslow, Abraham. *Motivation and Personality*. New York: Harper & Row, 1954.

Moore, Colin. *Behavioral Influences on Investment Decisions*: A Putnam Perspective February 2002.

Odean, Terrance. "What I Know About How You Invest." Presentation to Legg Mason Funds Management Investment Conference, Nov. 7–8, 2003, Las Vegas, Nevada.

———. "Are Investors Reluctant to Realize Their Losses?," *Journal of Finance* 53 (Oct. 2000): 1775–98.

O'Loughlin, James. *The Real Warren Buffett: Managing Capital, Leading People*. London: Nicholas Brealey Publishing, 2003.

Pape, Scott. *The Barefoot Investor: Five Steps to Financial Freedom*, 2nd ed. Melbourne: Pluto Press, 2007.

Ricard, Matthieu. *Happiness: A Guide to Developing Life's Most Important Skill.* London: Atlantic Books, 2007.

Schwartz, Barry. *The Paradox of Choice: Why More Is Less.* New York: Harper Perennial, 2005.

Schnarch, David. *Passionate Marriage: Keeping Love and Intimacy Alive in Committed Relationships.* New York: Owl Books, 1998.

Schroeder, Alice. *The Snowball: Warren Buffett and the Business of Life.* London: Bloomsbury, 2008.

Seligman, Martin. *Authentic Happiness: Using the New Positive Psychology to Realise Your Potential for Lasting Fulfilment.* Sydney: Random House Australia, 2002.

Sharp, Timothy. *The Happiness Handbook: Strategies for a Happy Life.* Sydney: Finch Publishing, 2005.

Shefrin, Hersch. *Beyond Greed and Fear: Understanding Behavioral Finance and the Psychology of Investing.* Cambridge, Mass.: Harvard Business School Press, 2000.

Shiller, Robert. *Irrational Exuberance.* New York: Currency, 2004.

———. Shiller, Robert. "Poor Are Richer and Climbing the Ladder Too," *Australian Financial Review* (Nov. 17, 2006): 75.

Statman, Meir, and Jonathan Scheid. "Buffett in Foresight and Hindsight," *Financial Analysts Journal* (July/Aug. 2002): 11–18.

Taleb, Nassim Nicholas. *Fooled by Randomness: The Hidden Role of Chance in the Markets and in Life.* New York: Texere, 2001.

Thaler, Richard H., and Shlomo Benartzi (2004) "Save More Tomorrow: Using Behavioral Economics to Increase Employee Saving," *Journal of Political Economy* 112, no. 1 (Feb. 2004): S164–S187.

Thaler, Richard H., Amos Tversky, Daniel Kahneman, and Alan Schwartz. "The Effect of Myopia and Loss-Aversion on Risk-Taking: An Experimental Test," *The Quarterly Journal of Economics* (May 1997).

Time magazine. Special Mind & Body Issue—The Science of Happiness (Jan. 17, 2005).

Tyndale, Philippa. *Don't Look Back: The David Bussau Story: How an Abandoned Child Became a Champion of the Poor.* Sydney: Allen & Unwin, 2004.

Wilson, Valerie. *The Secret Life of Money: Exposing the Private Parts of Personal Money.* Sydney: Allen & Unwin, 1999.

Woodward, Bob. *State of Denial*. New York: Simon & Schuster, 2006.

Yunus, Muhammad, with Alan Jolis. "Banker to the Poor: Micro-Lending and the Battle Against World Poverty." New York: Public Affairs, 1999. Accessed at www.muhammadyunus.org.

YWCA. *Beauty at Any Cost*. Washington, DC: YWCA, 2008.

INDEX

ABOUT THE AUTHORS

ARUN ABEY AND ANDREW FORD share a passion for helping people enjoy better lives by identifying their values and goals, and putting clear financial strategies in place to achieve them. With demanding careers and growing families, they both grapple with "how much is enough?" on a daily basis.

Arun Abey cofounded the international lifestyle financial planning firm ipac securities which has enjoyed twenty five years of uninterrupted growth. Key to its success has been the philosophy of building long-term relationships to help its clients discover and achieve their most important lifestyle goals. He is a noted strategic thinker whose views are often sought in the corporate world and widely quoted in the media. After the sale of ipac to AXA Asia Pacific, Arun remained Executive Chairman of ipac and took on the role of Head of Strategy for AXA.

He coauthored the international best seller *Fortune Strategy*, described by the *Financial Review* as one of the best books published on investment.

Arun graduated with "First Class Honours" in arts and economics from the Australian National University, is a fellow of the Financial Services Institute of Australia, and worked in economic research before starting ipac.

Andrew Ford, a marketing and communications expert, has held senior roles in the financial services and publishing industries in Australia and the United Kingdom.

Andrew has a bachelor's in economics from the University of Sydney. He started his career as a business and finance journalist, working across a diverse range of stock market and industry titles. He moved into marketing management within the publishing industry, ran his own financial communications consultancy for seven years, and is currently head of marketing for ipac securities.

Along the way, Andrew has written a 250-page stock market education course and *A Beginner's Guide to the Stock Market* (the latter for the top-selling magazine *Shares*), and he has edited and contributed to numerous books including *Retire Rich, Retire Early*.